UNDERSTANDING
AFRICA

D1409001

UNDERSTANDING AFRICA

A Political Economy Perspective

Richard A. Fredland
*Indiana University—Purdue University
Indianapolis*

Burnham Inc., Publishers

Chicago

President: Kathleen Kusta
Vice-President: Brett J. Hallongren
General Manager: Richard O. Meade
Project Editor: Sheila Whalen
Design/Production: Tamra Campbell-Phelps
Cover: "Wazzi, Cameroon" by Lois Coren
Photo Researcher: Randall Nicholas

Library of Congress Cataloging-in-Publication Data

Fredland, Richard A.
    Understanding Africa : a political economy perspective / Richard A. Fredland.
       p.   cm.
    ISBN 0-8304-1563-7 (pbk. : alk. paper)
    1. Africa—Economic conditions.   2. Africa—Economic policy.
3. Africa—Politics and government.   4. Colonies—Africa.
I. Title.
HC800F73   1999
330.96—dc21   99-37891
                                       CIP

Manufactured in the United States of America

The paper used in this book meets the minimum requirements of American National Standard for Information Sciences—Permanence of Paper for Printed Library Materials, ANSI Z39.48-1984.

Contents

CONTENTS

CONTENTS

CHAPTER 1

Introduction

This book originated during my year as a Fulbright Scholar at the University of Malawi. Its roots, however, are found in numerous years of study and in my extensive travels and research in many African countries. Consequently, my examples will reflect those experiences; nevertheless I believe I have maintained a broad perspective and have kept all examples generally applicable (though I recognize their limitations).

The following appeared in a foreword of an earlier volume I wrote. It is as timely today as when it first appeared:

Dam construction near Mekelle in Tigray Province, Ethiopia. Lack of both technical expertise and machinery means that even major construction projects are heavily dependent on human labor.

And the one who is addressed, the African, is asked no
questions. Freedom? Equal rights? "Yes, but only when
you have been baptized in the name of Christianity, in
the name of democracy, in the name of civilization, in
the name of economics, in the name of communism . . .
according to the particular faith in question. For all
these gods are the children of one who says: 'I am the
Lord . . . and thou shalt!'"

Map 1.1

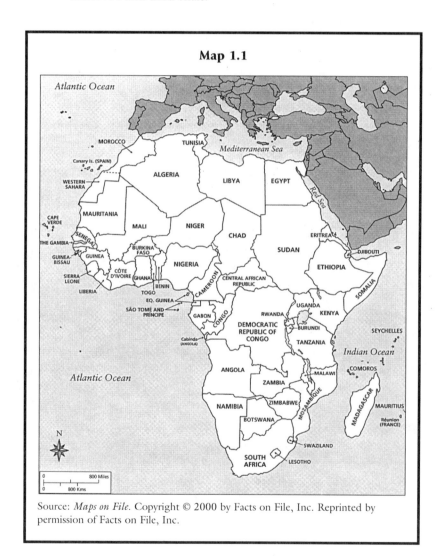

Source: *Maps on File.* Copyright © 2000 by Facts on File, Inc. Reprinted by
permission of Facts on File, Inc.

INTRODUCTION

> Plans are elaborated, programmes made, books written as to what should be opened up, in what direction it should be led. But the Africans are for the most part ignored. Nearly everyone who writes, speaks, arranges, recommends—disposes of them, because he thinks: "I am . . . and thou shalt!" (Janheinz Jahn, *Muntu: An Outline of the New African Culture*, 235)

Africa can be enigmatic, particularly for those who have been inattentive to its evolution or for those who resist coming to terms with something very different or new. But for anyone with a modicum of curiosity, Africa is a fascinating, complex, and infuriating place. Above all, understanding it requires a context—e.g., African literature, African anthropology, African culture. Africa, in all its complexity, constitutes a context. Thus, one might argue that once a coherent perspective has been established, one can begin to "understand" Africa. Perhaps this is so, perhaps not.

There are those who contend that one cannot understand Africa if one has not experienced personally the marginalization that has befallen Third World peoples at various times and places. If I believed that, I would not be writing these words. If the reader will permit the analogy, I assert that being peripheralized is like becoming a mother; it follows that though men cannot become mothers, they can become gynecologists by undergoing education and by acquiring experience. Likewise, one can intellectually "understand" Africa without being an African.

The study of Africa should not be confused with Afro-American or Black studies; rather, it should be seen as an area study comparable to the study of Latin America or China. As we do in any academic pursuit, we must make every effort to dissociate ourselves from our emotions while observing the phenomenon we seek to understand. While this should be self-evident in an academic setting, it is, in fact, difficult to separate African studies from race, the diaspora, and all their emotional implications. Most Africans are black, and they constitute marginalized populations in too many places. Further complicating objectivity—especially for Americans—the serious study of Africa was popularized in the 1960s when human rights issues were at the forefront of international politics, and civil rights issues were preeminent in the United States. In the minds of some observers, then, the two issues are inextricable. Of course, in the background of any study of Africa lies the topic of slavery, the cause of the diaspora and a major feature in the distortion of African culture, both on the continent and elsewhere.

Willie Abraham reminds us that Africans have the same problem we all have: "Objectivity requires externality." The implications for those who have little good to say about the "situation" in Africa may thus stem from misunderstandings of several sorts. The African response to many European "opportunities" was violent, especially from the viewpoint of the Europeans who dominated and consequently drafted the original versions of history. Yambo Ouologuem, an African intellectual, has argued that Africans have a duty to violence towards the whole pattern of misconceptions which for centuries reduced them to rabble. Just as wholesale condemnation of African systems arises from the excesses of the few, so a call for violence in reaction to perceived oppression may be acceptable to some in some circumstances, but as a standard it leaves much to be desired. The responsible scholar makes every effort to approach the topic with as much detachment as possible.

In approaching the specific study, one must keep in mind that facts constantly change, but concepts that evolve from theorizing are longer-lived. It is futile to *memorize* a great quantity of numbers, dates, and specifics. What we are seeking is an *understanding* of social—and especially of political and economic—processes that have created today's Africa and can simplify explaining it. Whether the population of country X is five or ten million is not of paramount importance, nor is its date of independence. From time to time it does become important to know that X became independent *before* Y, but that must be decided on a case-by-case basis.

The very attempt to understand a continent as large and diverse as Africa is presumptuous. Nonetheless, generalizations, however dangerous, are necessary if we are to reach any conclusions at all. So we enter this caveat at the outset: A statement such as "Africans are this" or "African governments do that" does not hold for *every* individual African nor for every African government.

An overriding reality which colors everything one can know about Africa, is reflected in figure 1.1.

Since it is impossible to keep track of every detail, we look for typologies and characterize how *most*, but not all, members of

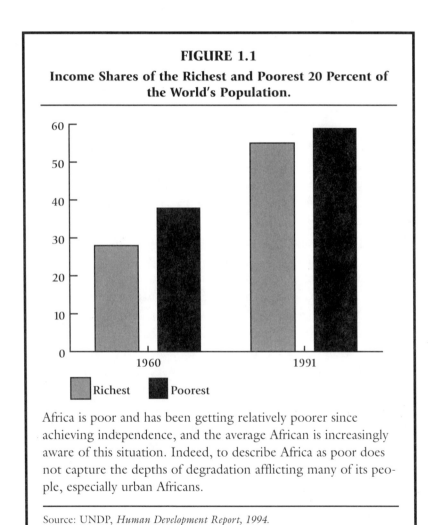

FIGURE 1.1

Income Shares of the Richest and Poorest 20 Percent of the World's Population.

Richest Poorest

Africa is poor and has been getting relatively poorer since achieving independence, and the average African is increasingly aware of this situation. Indeed, to describe Africa as poor does not capture the depths of degradation afflicting many of its people, especially urban Africans.

Source: UNDP, *Human Development Report, 1994.*

TABLE 1.1
Human Development Index

	GDP per Capita	HDI
Togo*	$1,167	.380
Portugal**	$12,674	.892

Source: Data from United Nations, *Human Development Report 1998*, I #128.
*The median African state.
**The median "high development" state.

the set we are examining behave. We try especially to take notice of the many differences which are apparent in African political systems: homogeneity versus heterogeneity, wealth versus poverty, stability versus instability, large versus small, Western versus Islamic versus eclectic, etc. Once again, we must be cautious about generalizations; most of our conclusions will be relative, not absolute.

This is not an apologia for Africa or for Africans. We will let the truth fall where it may, accepting the good news with the bad, examining positive judgments along with criticisms. The goal is not to persuade readers to agree, but to encourage insights into Africa that will help them better understand how and why Africa is as it is and allow them to develop their own conclusions.

Quantitatively, Africa is not a significant portion of the world: It represents 8–9 percent of the earth's population, a much smaller portion of the global gross national product, and less than 2 percent of global trade. To the extent that money matters, Africa does not. Measured on an alternative scale of human development, Africa does no better (see table 1.1). Yet it contains a large portion of the world's ethnic groups, fascinating flora and fauna, and some of the most wonderful people and places imaginable.

It has been my pleasure to study Africa for thirty-five years. During that period, I have come to realize how much there is to learn. On more than a few occasions, I have been forced— by changing facts and by my changing awareness of the facts—to alter my settled opinions. Be forewarned that this is likely to occur with any thoughtful observer. For example, ten years ago, it was inconceivable that Nelson Mandela would be freed from jail and within just a few months be elected President of South Africa (much less that his white predecessor would become a willing Vice President!) and all without a shot being fired.

Two organizing principles guide the thinking throughout this book, and both have subtexts. Together, they enable one to appreciate how Africa operates in today's world. This is not to suggest, of course, that they explain more than other variables, much less "everything" about Africa, or that the general principles suggested by other observers are wrong. Times change; understandings evolve; emphases differ. This is one person's considered perspective today on a very complex topic—no more. These are the two themes that I propose as key to "understanding" Africa.

The first organizing principle relates to the nature of the current international system. Since the demise of the Cold War, the international system has become more overtly dominated by economic considerations, as opposed to political or ideological ones, than at any time since World War II. The contemporary international economic system is essentially capitalist. Even when a more coherent anticapitalist bloc acted as a superpower, global economic interactions were driven not by the needs of the recipients, as communist theory would have it, but by the economic power of the dominant forces. That is, the Soviets were as interested as any capitalist in profiting from international transactions. They just cloaked their activities in more political bombast.

And Africa is a participant—willing or not—in the international capitalist system.

The second organizing principle relates to internal social structure as it determines the nature of the economic **marketplace** and the accompanying political structure. Aside from a few exceptions (e.g., oil in Nigeria; diamonds, cobalt, gold, and copper in southern Africa; and bauxite in Ghana), there are few "hard" materials with which Africa can bargain in an open marketplace. Hence, Africa finds itself peripheralized in the global economy. On the "soft" side, the continent has tourism through safaris—for as long as game can roam without being displaced by settlement—a few beaches, and a warm climate, all assets as long as tourists feel safe in taking advantage of these attractions. These "comparative advantages," however, are not the makings of an economic powerhouse.

MARKETPLACE

This term is usually associated with business or economics, but it is crucial to understanding Africa. It implies an open economic situation in which buyers and sellers operate freely. Nothing can be sold if there is no market, regardless of the price or availability of a commodity. In Africa, there is no market for cream puffs, Rolls Royces, or new Gucci shoes. Not surprisingly, there is no supply either. There is, however, an extensive potential market for foodstuffs of various sorts, but there is also a very restricted supply because there are *no resources* to chase after the supply. Even when a commodity is in abundant supply or oversupply, if there are no funds to chase after the goods, there is no market. This basic economic concept explains much African behavior. If a market is demonstrated in peanuts, carved bowls, or fish, immediately salespersons appear in droves.

Peasants are not immune to basic economic reality. Depressingly, most African countries have labor surpluses, so the "market" in human services is at the buyers' discretion. This is why a servant working a seventy-hour week may be paid thirty dollars. If the first paid applicant refuses this meager wage, a desperate second or third is willing to accept it.

The market, then, determines the behavior of a substantial portion of people in Africa (not to mention elsewhere).

BOX 1.1

INTRODUCTION

In the international political system in which one dominates or is dominated, Africans do not dominate. They are the recipients—some would say victims—of the vagaries of a system in which they are nonconsenting participants. One must see Africa's relationship to the international political-economic system in order to understand how the continent participates in the world.

Regarding internal social structure, there are two considerations, one major and the other subsidiary. What central organizing principal, focused on a capitalist international system, is the foremost implicit consideration in social activity in the West? Without being too Marxian, I would suggest that it is materialism and its close ally, the principle of efficiency. As a general rule, the West prizes material accomplishment above all else. Other values may be associated, but they are secondary. Efficiency requires, and results from, organizing resources according to clear-cut priorities and from a readiness to invest resources—whether of time, money, or talent—in order to produce something more valuable in the future.

Many Africans, however, have little and see themselves potentially acquiring even less. Needing so much, they cannot think about being efficient. They want to garner what they can—in this sense they are certainly materialists—but they cannot and will not risk the little that they have on the chance of creating more. The image that comes to my mind is of a market woman alongside a road with her small stack of fruits or vegetables. I have often seen, across African cultures, such women stack and restack a few lemons, groundnuts, or green peppers, apparently savoring the value of the inventory and the prospect of garnering a few coins. This vendor is usually seated only a few feet from another woman who is selling the same lemons, doing the same rearranging. There is no apparent sense of competition—that is not the African way—and there is an inherent reserve in the fact that risks are avoided. And so African society avoids both the unpleasantness of competition and confrontation, and the attendant savings accounts!

CHAPTER 1

That African societies have developed in this way is easily understood, but such understanding does not make life more productive. The necessity of operating on such slender margins prevents Africans, for the most part, from practicing "deferred gratification"—that is, postponing consumption to a future time while saved resources earn interest and are available to others to borrow for investment in an economically better tomorrow. This is *not* the African way. These operating principles drive much social organization in Africa and can be expected to be operative until comprehensive transformations take place.

This book aims to make Africa comprehensible to the generally informed reader who has not had years of preparatory study. After reading it, you should be able to approach a news report on a contemporary African topic (all too often negative in the Western media) and fit it into a larger picture. You will not be prepared to write a dissertation, teach a course, or even make a trip. But should you plan to do any of these, this book will be a valuable starting point.

No serious study can be undertaken until preconceptions and prejudices are set aside or at least suspended. The study of Africa is no different. Approach this topic with a *tabula rasa* till the case has been made. Then return to your preconceptions and see if they are still appropriate. Or formulate more accurate ones.

Both training and experience are important. The best experience undoubtedly comes from the actuality of Africa itself—walking the streets of Dakar, eating *nsima* in Malawi, or rejoicing in the unparalleled beauty of Cape Town from atop Table Mountain. However, since most readers are unlikely to have such opportunities, understanding must be sought through conventional academic avenues—books, articles and, yes, the Internet. Indeed, this book does not contain my own final conclusions, only today's considered opinion! Tomorrow I could be compelled to change my mind in the face of newly discovered facts or modified insights. Only time will tell.

Meanwhile, read and enjoy!

A NOTE ON EPISTEMOLOGY

In our age of overwhelming information supply, it is tempting to think that we know all we need to know. After all, we have access to 24-hour television news, instantaneous reportage of world events, and endless interpretation of those events.

However, before we come to that conclusion, we need to consider the information we receive and how we receive it. One cliché describes television reporting, "If it bleeds, it leads." Experience tells us that importance is not the criterion for media reporting; the major focus of reporting is on whatever will capture people's attention, since reporting—at least in the United States—is a business. So one rule of news production is that it must make money for the provider. Naturally, then, coverage of Africa will emphasize bleeding. A constitutional conference culminating in a bloodless revolution in South Africa is unquestionably more significant than a terrorist murder, but it is far less telegenic.

A second limitation on news is availability. Remember the philosopher's conundrum about whether the tree falling in the forest makes a sound if no one hears it? If events in the real world are not recorded by the media, did they really happen? If we don't hear about them, we cannot take them into consideration in our own thinking. Africa is far from the center of the world of international media, and much that transpires there goes unreported.

Psychological considerations are also important: As an observer, I can report only what I am able to see. A student of African cultures might recognize the ethnic content of a political dispute while an untrained observer would see nothing more than primitive chaos. Also, individuals who make the news can use psychological techniques to affect the message—"spinning," as the process is described in contemporary Washington politics and media. The political leader who stands in front of new construction and boasts of his accomplishments may be distorting his record without *saying* anything untrue.

None of these deficiencies stems from malicious behavior.

CONCEPT BOXES

When a crucial term or idea first appears in the text, it is accompanied by a *concept box* explaining its relevance in the context of this book. These are not definitions; they are discussions of ideas integral to "understanding Africa" from an international and political-economic perspective.

Why are concept boxes important? An infinite number of facts about Africa can be amassed, but they will be useless unless they are set into a framework for assessing their significance. The concept boxes provide such a framework.

The first term, *marketplace,* for example, is a concept, that can be broadly interpreted to explain political and social exchanges as well as economic ones. The explanation in the box offers the reader an interpretation of the term as it applies to this book.

The same is true of the concept boxes that follow. Books could be, and have been, written about virtually every one of these topics, so if a specific topic particularly interests you, it can be more fully investigated.

(Concept boxes are included in the table of contents.)

BOX 1.2

Instead, individuals do their jobs as their environments demand, but there are some who would distort reality for their own purposes. Both sides did this—though to widely disparate degrees—during the Cold War, and their fears or hopes often colored the news we were given.

Because Africa is economically insignificant, geographically remote, and exceedingly complex, it is not surprising that we get only fragmentary information from the popular media. We can overcome this in our own lives by paying more attention to events on that continent. First, however, we must have a background for putting events into context. This book seeks to provide that background.

CHAPTER 2

Before the Present Age: History and Geography

L et's not forget "context": One's understandings come in the context of one's knowledge and experiences; hence the parable of the blind men and the elephant.[1] All the blind men were correct based on their differing experiences; but none could really transmit an accurate understanding of an elephant because of their limited perspectives. So it is with Africa. Have you heard someone say: "I met a Frenchman/Mexican/Burmese/Malawian once, and

The colonial era left African states with Western models of governance despite dramatic cultural differences. Here, Kenyan President Daniel Arap Moi reviews his troops outside the parliament building in Nairobi.

I don't like the French/Mexicans/Burmese/Malawians"? The very title of this book—Understanding Africa—encourages just such generalizations. "Africa" is a complex set of human interactions; so understanding Africa actually implies understanding several Africas on several levels.

A student once came to me following a class discussion in this vein and recounted his first—and only—visit to Africa. He was in the U.S. military aboard a ship in the Mediterranean. The day came when he was to helicopter to "Africa" for training. He produced a photograph of the first African he saw, a Berber (probably) shepherd in Morocco or Tunisia. Other things aside, the color of this "African" was not what the student expected; he was not black as Africans were supposed to be. The student immediately realized that his experience of growing up in a small town in the Midwest had not prepared him for such nuances—that there could possibly be an African—Africans?—of his own Midwestern skin hue! Still, we can be reasonably comfortable with the term black Africa because it does capture the color of the vast majority of Africans south of the Sahara, but we must keep in mind that Africa is extraordinarily diverse.

The first step toward "understanding" Africa, then, is to acknowledge the epistemological questions: "What do we know?" and "How do we know it?" We all know that Africans are black; that is simply a fact (as long as we do not quibble about what constitutes "black"—e.g., charcoal versus mahogany). But, as my student's experience demonstrated, there is more to the question than that. Several facts are true about the color of Africans: For instance, a South African of Dutch descent whose family has been African for three hundred years is very likely blue-eyed and blond-haired. So, for starters, we must recognize that facts about Africa must be put into context and examined for nuances. That done, we can proceed to work on *understanding Africa*.

Well, almost. At some point we need to catch up on postindependence name changes. When I mention that I teach African politics, non-scholars often ask, "How can you possibly

TABLE 2.1

Postindependence Name Changes

Current Name	Former Name(s)	Date(s) of Change
Benin	Dahomey	1975 (Traditional name)
Burkina Faso	Upper Volta	1984 (Traditional name)
Central African Republic	Central African Empire	1979 (Short-lived name change)
Côte d'Ivoire	Ivory Coast	Colonial name. Ivory Coast was taken at independence and revised in 1988.
Democratic Republic of the Congo	Congo-Leopoldville Zaire	1. 1971 (Traditional name) 2. 1997 (Mobutu-era authenticité)
Eritrea, Ethiopia	Ethiopia	1995 (Separation)
Namibia	South West Africa	1976–1993
Republic of South Africa	Union of South Africa	1961 (Left the Commonwealth)
Tanzania	Tanganyika, Zanzibar	1964 (Merger)
Zimbabwe	Zimbabwe-Rhodesia	1965–1979 (Interim regime)

keep up with all the changes?" For those who have already mastered Slovenia, Slovakia, and Tadjikistan, Mumbai and Myanmar, here is what has changed in Africa since 1960; you will see that the name changes, at least, have been minimal (see table 2.1).

The beginning of an understanding of Africa comes with two verities which are essentially unalterable: its history and its geography. Let's examine the latter first.

GEOGRAPHY

On the map, Africa is a continent of substantial size—second only to Asia in area. What the map does not show, however, is that in other than geographic terms there are actually two Africas. Politically, historically, and culturally, Africa is divided roughly into the Arab/Muslim North and the Bantu/black South—but even this statement requires caveats. Consequently, when one discusses Africa in an academic context, one usually means "sub-Saharan" Africa, excluding the five states of the "Maghreb"—Morocco, Tunisia, Algeria, Libya, and Egypt. These states are indeed African geographically, but they are predominantly Middle Eastern culturally: The Maghreb states are Arab and Moslem and were formerly part of the Ottoman Empire. This is how they view themselves, and they orient their international activities more toward the Middle East than toward Africa.

This distinction is not accepted by all observers. For example, some would argue that the first African civilization was in Egypt and are not willing to consign Egypt to the Middle East. In the interest of keeping this book culturally and politically coherent, however, I shall deal only with the 47 African states located south of the Sahara.[2]

One challenge a writer on this subject faces is the need to keep a proper perspective in terms of details—presenting neither too many nor too few. First, Africa is large—three times the size of the United States with perhaps twice its population. It is, in Ali Mazrui's words, "firmly central" on the globe, the only continent crossed by both the Tropics of Cancer and Capricorn (p. 116). Its location provides much of the continent with tropical weather and year-round moderate or warm temperatures. The Sahara, however, can experience a greater temperature range within a day than the rest of the continent sees over an entire year. Given its mountains, deserts, forests, and large rivers, Africa is not coherent; it has been physically divided since it first appeared, tectonically separated from Godwana in the misty past.

The best-defined physical division is the Rift Valley which extends from the Red Sea in the North through the major lakes of East and Central Africa till it fades beyond the southern end of Lake Malawi, some five thousand kilometers to the south. The valley, which can be readily seen near the equator in Kenya, is a submerged segment of a tectonic plate, and it constitutes a formidable barrier to travel in its region. The waters of Lake Tanganyika—whose surface is about 1000 meters above sea level—are over 1700 meters deep; elsewhere the valley presents 800-meter escarpments and is 35 to 100 kilometers wide. With a temperature differential of 1 degree celsius per hundred meters of elevation change, the valley is much warmer than the surrounding plateau.

Major mountain ranges also create barriers to the free flow of people and commodities: The Atlas Mountains, the southeastern extension of the Alps, divide Morocco into a coastal plain and a high plateau. More impressive still is the Drakensburg massif in the eastern high-veld region of South Africa, encompassing all of Lesotho. Snow-covered three-thousand-meter peaks abound. The Eastern plateau (Kenya and surrounds) lies at about 2,000 meters and the Ethiopian highlands rise to over 4,000 meters. Other mountains include Kilimanjaro, perennially snow-topped even though it is practically on the Equator in Tanzania. The "great lakes region" (Rwanda, Uganda, etc.) is also mountainous.

Deserts of barren rock and vast stretches of sand are another geographic feature that divides the continent. The Sahara comprises all or part of the five Maghreb states plus major portions of Mauritania, Mali, Niger, Chad, Sudan, and Burkina Faso. Rainfall at Timbuktu, for example, does not exceed 30 centimeters annually, compared to over three times that amount in the midwestern United States. Elevations reach 3,300 meters, and in a single day the temperature may vary 30 degrees celsius. Though it reaches back centuries, the Sahara expanded aggressively in the 1970s, a result of both climatological and human causes. That great desert is a major feature, and marginal areas (the Sahel) surrounding it constitute virtually all the land area in these and several other countries. The other major desert is the Kalahari/Namib which constitutes most of Namibia and Botswana and major portions of South Africa. Arid regions are also found in northern Kenya and Ethiopia. Because of the combination of aridity, heat, tropical rains, and rocks, only 8 percent of Africa's land area is arable in the conventional agricultural sense. Contrary to general impressions, deserts are not just dry sand; there are water holes (oases) and much of the Sahara is rock. In fact, if the appropriate balance between water inflow and water use is maintained, it is possible for the Sahara to sustain some grazing.

At the other extreme is the rainforest, which may accumulate 160 to over 400 centimeters of rain annually. The accompanying humidity makes life uncomfortable, fosters the growth of organisms that destroy paper as well as crops, and causes a variety of maladies in people and animals. Mosquito-borne malaria is endemic in much of Africa, disabling residents and proving fatal in millions of cases. The presence of the tsetse fly has rendered much of Africa inhospitable to domesticated farm animals and has transmitted sleeping sickness to humans, but now research is finding ways to cope with this pest.[3]

Rivers have traditionally provided protection from invaders as well as invasion routes, but they also present barriers to trade and the sharing of culture and ideas. Africa is estimated to have 40 percent of the world's hydroelectric potential in its rivers, but less than 2 percent of it is developed. The Zaire River alone—which traverses northern Congo (Zaire) in a great swoop of 2,500 kilometers—contains one-sixth of the world's hydroelectric potential in that one stream, equivalent to the combined hydroelectric potential of all the waters in the United States (Hochschild, p. 17). Though rivers also serve as a transportation medium, this use of the Congo is constrained by the 350 kilometers of rapids at Kinshasa-Brazzaville, some 120 kilometers from the ocean.[4] Add to that the Nile (with its Blue and White tributaries) which flows northward for 6,500 kilometers, losing water to evaporation as it meanders through Sudan and Egypt, dropping no more than 120 meters in 1,300 kilometers. Three-quarters of its flow comes in the wet season of August–November. So precious is its water, that 90 percent of Egypt's population is crowded into its valley. The Limpopo and Zambezi Rivers (the latter pouring over Victoria Falls) flow in and near Mozambique; the Niger (over 4,000 kilometers long), the Senegal (1,500 kilometers), and the Volta Rivers traverse West Africa. These and other rivers contribute to Africa's segmentation while offering only limited transportation.

From a geologic perspective one must note the insufficiency of Africa's soils. Consider the extensive deserts; the arid, steppe-like conditions of much of East Africa; the untillable mountains; the rainforest; and other regions where regular deluges deplete the soil of nutrition. This precludes any agriculture beyond **subsistence** farming, and reduces timberable trees in some areas to

---

SUBSISTENCE

Subsistence is bare survival; it characterizes the lives of people who work but never accumulate material possessions—e.g., peasants in Africa and elsewhere. Their primary economic activity is barter, so individuals do not amass an economic surplus for taking care of their own unexpected needs, much less for purchases or investment. A subsistence farmer may have "pocket change" with which to purchase seeds, salt, and sugar, but not enough for clothes, medicines, school fees, or other second-tier necessities, and certainly not for luxuries.

BOX 2.1

---

as few as one per three-to-four acres; despite this, timbering is rapidly reducing rainforest area, and there is, not surprisingly, virtually no pro-environment activity in impoverished states. Geologically, Africa's bedrock may contain substantial amounts of iron and aluminum. There are rich veins of gold, copper, diamonds, cobalt, and other minerals in the Congo (Zaire)-Zimbabwe-Botswana-South Africa region. From a mineralogical perspective, South Africa is also a major world player except for its lack of oil; it is a major food exporter and a financial powerhouse as well, and it has developed a technique for extracting oil from coal.

Then there are the geographic distances. Africa is a large place; the Congo (Zaire) alone is comparable in size to the United States east of the Mississippi River. Given such great distances and the various topographical barriers already noted, Africa is clearly ripe for division. Think of the triangle formed by Atlanta, St. Louis, and Boston. If one superimposed that triangle on Europe, it would encompass Madrid, Copenhagen, and Istanbul, virtually all of Western Europe. Impose it on Africa, however, and the distance from the northern border of South Africa to Cape Town approximates the distances from Boston to Atlanta or Copenhagen to Istanbul. What's more, fifteen of Africa's states are landlocked, dependent upon others for access to the sea for trade. These factors help to explain—at least in part—Africa's impoverishment.

Physical Africa is interesting, daunting, awesome. The combination of mountains, desert, plateaus, the Rift Valley with its lakes, the mighty rivers, and the rainforest creates an enormous diversity of topography. Unfortunately, what one sees is not exactly what one gets. The very fertile-looking, rain-soaked lands of the tropics are actually relatively infertile, because the excessive rains leach nutrients from the soil. Productive agriculture in such locations requires substantial inputs of fertilizer and careful selection of seeds.

The dramatic seasonal shifts in rain inland from Madagascar produce a rainy season in which two or more meters of rain may fall in a few months. This is followed by a dry period in which lakes and streams dry up and lack of water becomes a serious problem. North of there as much as 40 percent of the savannah regions may burn every year, set alight by both lightning strikes and human carelessness. The savannah, like the desert, comes in several versions—cooled by the elevations west of the Rift Valley in Eastern Africa, tropical and hot to the west. Plant growth is so fragile that the savannah is easily converted to desert by slight overgrazing. Even a few trips across it in a vehicle will turn the track into permanent desert. The temperature is as high as that of the rainforest, without the humidity.

The twenty inches of annual rainfall is insufficient to enable this fragile ecosystem to recover. At the same time, the combination of a bit more rain and moderating ocean currents produce a pleasant and fertile Mediterranean climate for South Africa's coast.

As Africa's population has mushroomed, people searching for wood for cooking fires or grazing land for animals (goats, cattle, camels) have destroyed extensive stretches of the savannah, driving its inhabitants further and further into marginal regions. As this cycle is replicated over and over, the continent is exceeding its **carrying capacity**. The data in table 2.2 show the way

CARRYING CAPACITY

Carrying capacity is the ability of a given area of land to support life. A grazing animal, for example, requires X area in a given climatic region in order to thrive. A different animal or a different region would change the calculus. The temptation, especially among the unaware or the unconcerned, is to push carrying capacity to and beyond its limit, creating what is generally termed the "tragedy of the commons" because owners of animals grazing on commonly-held land tend to exceed its carrying capacity. Too many animals grazing on a given space will starve.

BOX 2.2

Africa is losing ground economically as a result of population growth outstripping economic growth.

In order to stay even, economic growth and population growth must be equal or economic growth must be greater, but there are only two examples of that—Botswana and Lesotho with Swaziland almost even.

Africa's transportation **infrastructure** is substantially underdeveloped; portions which were built during the colonial era have fallen into disrepair or been destroyed as a result of military or

TABLE 2.2

GDP and Population Growth Rates

State	1 Annual Population Growth Rate Percent 1970–1995	2 GDP per capita, annual rate of change 1960–1995	3 Difference between population and GDP growth rates ( ) indicates greater population growth rate
Angola	2.7	−2.6	(5.3)
Benin	2.8	0.4	(2.4)
Botswana	3.3	6.1	2.8
Burkina Faso	2.7	1.2	(1.5)
Burundi	2.2	1.1	(1.1)
Cameroon	2.8	0.5	(2.3)
CAR	2.3	−0.5	(2.8)
Chad	2.2	−0.4	(2.6)
Congo	2.9	1.6	(1.3)
Cote d'Ivoire	3.7	1.1	(2.6)
Djibouti	5.8	—	—
Eritrea	2.2	—	—
Ethiopia	2.7	−1.2	(3.9)
Gabon	3.1	1.3	(1.8)
Gambia	3.6	1.1	(2.5)
Ghana	2.8	−0.5	(3.3)
Guinea	2.6	1.1	(1.5)
Guinea-Bissau	2.9	0.2	(2.7)
Kenya	3.5	1.6	(1.9)
Lesotho	2.6	3.8	0.8
Madagascar	3.1	−1.5	(4.6)
Malawi	3.1	1.0	(2.1)

civil unrest. North of South Africa, there is only a single rail link across the continent—from Angola to Mozambique—and this was damaged and disrupted during civil wars in both those places in the 1970s and 1980s. Only recently has an all-weather highway been completed, crossing the continent from Lagos to Mombasa. Unfortunately, despite thousands of miles of coastline, there are only a few good ports—Djibouti, Dar Es Salaam, Cape Town, Dakar. Transportation infrastructure is oriented to these locations, causing congestion and overconcentration. To further complicate the devel-

TABLE 2.2
(Continued)

State	1 *Annual Population Growth Rate Percent 1970–1995*	2 *GDP per capita, annual rate of change 1960–1995*	3 *Difference between population and GDP growth rates ( ) indicates greater population growth rate*
Mali	2.8	0.5	(2.3)
Mauritania	2.5	1.0	(1.5)
Mozambique	2.5	0.2	(2.3)
Namibia	2.7	−0.8	(3.5)
Niger	3.2	−2.0	(5.2)
Nigeria	2.9	0.2	(2.7)
Senegal	2.8	−0.2	(3.0)
Sierra Leone	1.9	1.0	(0.9)
South Africa	2.5	0.5	(3.0)
Sudan	2.7	-0.1	(2.8)
Swaziland	2.9	2.8	(0.1)
Tanzania	3.2	0.4	(2.8)
Togo	2.9	0.8	(2.1)
Uganda	2.8	1.6	(1.2)
Zaire	3.3	−2.0	(5.3)
Zambia	2.7	−1.3	(4.0)
Zimbabwe	3.1	0.8	(2.3)

Sources: *Human Development Report 1998*, UNDP. Data in column 1 from table 22, for 1970–1995; in column 2, table 6, for 1960–1995. Consequently, the calculated annual differences in column 3 are artifices and are not arithmetically accurate. They do, however, indicate that the *general* trend has been overwhelmingly toward populations growing faster than GDPs. By the calculations in this table, per-capita GDP has outpaced population growth in only two of 37 states for which there are full data.

INFRASTRUCTURE

In every society physical elements constitute the means by which people participate in the distribution of goods. Constructing infrastructure is a large part of what development is about. Infrastructure is generally thought of as bridges, hospitals, telephone systems, and manufacturing facilities. It represents both an investment in resources and access to the requisite technology. A state's level of infrastructure is loosely taken as a measure of its modernity—that is, a society with no airline or radio stations is not seen as being very modern.

At the time of independence, there was rudimentary infrastructure in place in most colonies except the Belgian Congo, but when the French in Guinea and the Portuguese departed, they did all they could to render infrastructure useless. For example, they poured cement into water pipes and removed telephone wires.

BOX 2.3

opment of workable African transportation, most infrastructure development retains its colonial orientation to the major city or port and does not facilitate travel to neighboring areas.

HISTORY

Africa's historic past is not easily traced; there are few written records, because paper was not in use even though it was invented in Egypt. As a consequence much of what is known about Africa comes from oral history, which contains its share of distortions just as written history does. Knowledge of Africa's past is gradually being expanded by archaeologists, serologists, linguists, and ethnologists.

The Romans and Greeks engaged in transactions with

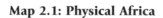

Map 2.1: Physical Africa

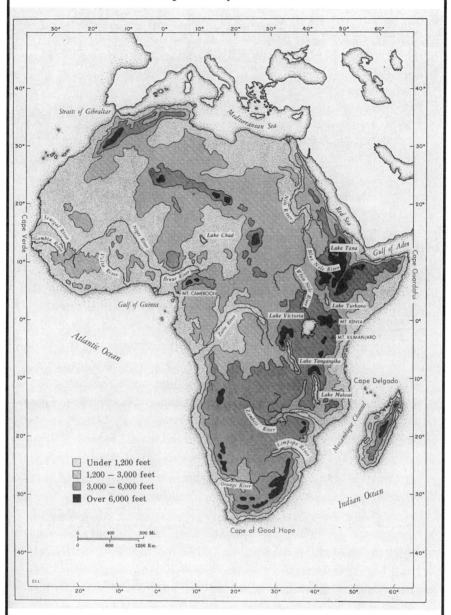

Source: Phyllis Martin and Patrick O'Meara, *Africa* (Bloomington: Indiana University Press, 1997), 39.

several African locations—present-day Egypt, Sudan, Somalia, Eritrea—establishing garrisons and colonies, one of which was called Africa by the Romans. Early Europeans entertained strange notions indeed:

> [A] Benedictine monk who mapped the world about 1350 claimed that Africa contained one-eyed people who used their feet to cover their heads. A geographer in the next century announced that the continent held people with one leg, three faces, and the heads of lions. (Hochschild, p. 6)

The modern age, in terms of Western civilization, came to much of Africa in the late nineteenth century. This was politically confirmed in Berlin in 1884 when several European states met to divide up the continent. The late nineteenth century had seen a scramble for access to the presumed wealth of Africa (think of colonies such as the "Gold" Coast and "Ivory" Coast) as well as strategic access to the sea routes to the East which made the Cape of Good Hope so valuable. The scarcity of European contact with Africa prior to this time had given it such names as the dark continent or terra incognita in Europe. While central portions of Africa were indeed sparsely populated, Africa was hardly "dark" in the sense of being inactive in the international arena. Extensive kingdoms existed in the north, west, and south long before Europeans appeared. Table 2.3 sets out some major historical events, but these only hint at the breadth and depth of African history.

Long before the arrival of the Europeans, there were highly organized polities. Examples include Ghana (500–1300 CE) which at its zenith could put 200,000 mounted warriors in the field. Mali produced the trading center of Timbuktu with its university and its thriving commerce. The origins of Great Zimbabwe are still shrouded in mystery, but there is evidence of a substantial construction hundreds of years old.

For an understanding of contemporary Africa, however, the crucial historical periods are colonial and postcolonial. By 1900 all of Africa with the notable exceptions of Ethiopia and

Liberia was in the hands of European powers. While there were substantial differences in styles of colonial administration (about which more later), the general effect was to deprive Africa of its very soul.

The dominant colonial powers were Britain and France (see map 2.2), with Portugal, Germany, Belgium, and Italy far

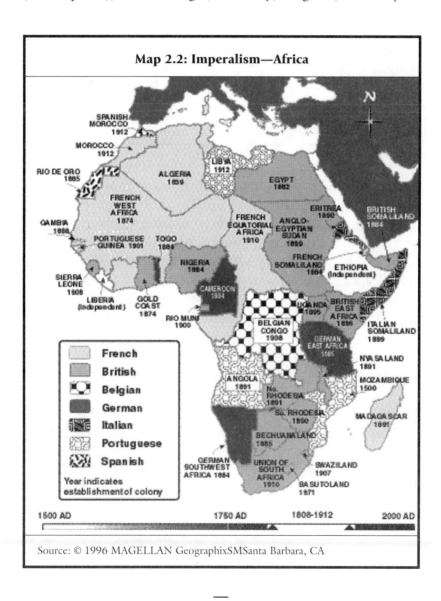

Map 2.2: Imperalism—Africa

Source: © 1996 MAGELLAN GeographixSMSanta Barbara, CA

COLONIES

The term specifies a relationship between a metropole and some other territory. The relationship is inherently exploitative because the colonizer extracts resources from the colonized though the process may be more or less humane and fair. Virtually all of Africa in the early and mid-twentieth century consisted of European colonies.

BOX 2.4

behind. **Colonies** were perceived to be sources of wealth, prestige, strategic naval and trading locations, and manpower for military and other activities. With few exceptions, there were no cities of any consequence in precolonial Africa, which meant there was little need for surplus production since virtually everyone was an agriculturalist until this century. The absence of surplus production obviates the need for storage, processing, and other survival practices that move civilization along. Nomads and pastoralists had little free time to develop complex cultural traditions.

No universal agreement has emerged regarding whether a large population is an asset or a liability. The primary resource that any society has is its people. Basically, nothing useful for humans happens in agriculture, education, or mining without human intervention, so it is axiomatic that a minimal population is required for a society to prosper. However, the question of "carrying capacity" is the other side of the coin. A few people are necessary, but a lot may not be better. Population is comparable to rainfall: without some, nothing happens; but too much is destructive.

Those who argue that many African states are overpopu-

TABLE 2.3

Important Dates in African History

7 million years ago—Hominids first emerge in Africa.

20,000 BCE—Bantu cultures arise in southern Africa.

10,000–3,000 BCE—Farming begins as lakes dry up around the Sahara.

3500 BCE—Nile states emerge.

3000 BCE—Egyptians produce food surpluses, making cities viable.

2000 BCE—Kingdom of Kush (Ethiopia) arises and is later vanquished by Axum.

600 BCE—Continent is first circumnavigated, according to Herodotus.

500 BCE—Asian food is introduced by Indian Ocean traders.

300 BCE—Great Greek city of Alexandria is founded, home of the famous library.

200 BCE—Rome establishes settlements in North Africa.

300 CE—Kingdom of Zimbabwe flourishes.

325 CE—Christian rulers come to power in Axum; iron is discovered in Zimbabwe (Great Zim).

500–1300 CE—Kingdom of Ghana arises; sends forth 200,000 warriors.

600–1500 CE—Kingdom of Songhai is established in West Africa.

639–681 CE—Moslems conquer North Africa; Islam slowly spreads southward and westward.

700 CE—Arabs colonize East Africa; slave trade begins.

1030 CE—Islam makes its way to Takrur in the Senegal River valley.

1150 CE—City of Timbuktu is founded, visited annually by 12,000 camels and chariots; kingdom of Mali arises and lasts until 1600; trans-Sahara trade is established in salt, gold, books; diplomatic relations are formalized among these kingdoms.

1200 CE—Egypt repels Mongols and Crusaders.

1300 CE—Pilgrimages to Mecca begin.

1350 CE—University is established in Timbuktu.

1415 CE—Portuguese trade begins; Prince Henry trades with Arabia, China, and India; Swahili language develops from Arabic.

1441 CE—Portugal takes its first slaves; England, Denmark, France, Holland, and Prussia follow suit.*

1481 CE—First Portuguese settle in Ghana; gold mining begins; Portuguese settle in Angola.

1486 CE—Diaz discovers Cape of Good Hope† and Portuguese settle there.

1491 CE—Catholic missionaries arrive in the Congo basin (Zaire).

TABLE 2.3 (CONTINUED)
Important Dates in African History

1505 CE—Portuguese settle in Mozambique.

1517 CE—Charles V of Spain licenses Flemish traders to import 4000 slaves annually to America.

1518 CE—First African bishop is named in the Congo.

1562 CE—British slave trade begins.

1633 CE—Portuguese missionaries are expelled from Abyssinia.

1652 CE—Dutch settle Cape Colony; East India Company is established.

Early 1700s CE—West African states develop: Asante, Yorubaland, Oyo; kingdom of Buganda is founded in East Africa; urban centers, many of them Moslem, emerge, and trade, and armies are established; use of firearms allows consolidation of power; confrontation develops among Islam, Christianity, and mercantilism.

1770 CE—James Bruce discovers the Nile junction and learns Arabic.

1787 CE—Sierra Leone Company is created by Britain to resettle slaves.

1795–1805 CE—Englishman Mungo Park explores the Senegal and Niger Rivers.

1806 CE—Britain occupies the Cape of Good Hope.

1807 CE—Britain declares the slave trade illegal.

1809 CE—Pass system for Hottentots is instituted by the Dutch, requiring indigenous Africans to carry identification and obtain permission for travel.

1814 CE—Cape Colony is ceded to England for $6 million.

1820–1830 CE—France conquers Algeria.

1823 CE—Liberia is founded to resettle American slaves.

1836–1840 CE—Great Boer trek moves Dutch into the Transvaal in what is to become South Africa.

1840 CE—First British arrive in Zanzibar and establish a consulate.

1843 CE—England annexes the Orange Free State.

1847 CE—Liberia becomes independent.

Mid-1800s CE—Stanley and Livingston cross Africa.

1869 CE—Suez Canal is opened; bought by Britain.

1875 CE—British East India Company gains a monopoly on trade with the East.‡

1877 CE—England annexes the Transvaal.

1880 CE—At least one-half of Africa's 11.5 million square miles are claimed by Europeans.

1880–1890 CE—Europeans scramble to establish colonies in Africa.

TABLE 2.3 (CONTINUED)
Important Dates in African History

1884 CE—**Congress of Berlin** convenes to satisfy Germany's
        need for colonies without a war.
1890s CE—Witwatersrand gold rush occurs in South Africa.
1896 CE—Menelik of Ethiopia defeats the Italians at Adowa.
1898 CE—The French confront the British at Khartoum in
        Sudan—and lose.

CONGRESS OF BERLIN

This international conference marked the culmination of the race for
colonies by major European powers and defined the epitome of
external control of Africa. It was attended by diplomats from England, Germany, Austria-Hungary, Belgium, Denmark, Spain, the
United States, France, Italy, Netherlands-Luxembourg, Portugal, Russia, Sweden-Norway, and the Ottoman Empire, but no African states.
It provided that:

1. Free trade would exist in the Congo basin.
2. No tax would be levied on imports into Africa.
3. The slave trade would be outlawed.
4. Protection for the church would be guaranteed.
5. Mediation was compulsory for all disputes in the Congo
   basin.
6. The Niger River was open to all.
7. A state had to prove effective occupation and make a formal announcement to establish a colony.
8. The "hinterland theory"—that occupation of the coast
   implied the right to the hinterland—was to be recognized.
9. King Leopold was to be sovereign in the Congo (which
   was annexed by Belgium in 1908).

Thus was Africa "sliced up" according to the colonizers'
notions and desires. As a consequence of the conference, Africa's
borders to this day are attributable to European preferences and not
to African realities.

BOX 2.5

TABLE 2.3 (CONTINUED)
Important Dates in African History

1905 CE—France, Britain, and Italy divide Somaliland.

1911 CE—Italy annexes Libya from the Ottoman Empire.

1919 CE—German colonies are mandated to France, Britain, Belgium, and South Africa by the League of Nations.

1931 CE—The Statute of Westminster establishes South Africa's independence.

1935 CE—Italy invades Ethiopia.

1940 CE—British Colonial Welfare and Development Act is passed.

1957 CE—Ghana receives its independence; the rest of the continent follows; the Conference of Independent African States is established.

DEMOCRACY

This is the popular term for a particular political culture. Simplistically, it is a system of government in which the citizens choose their leaders. But it is much more than that, especially in the African context. If it amounted simply to having elections, then a state could print ballots, hold an election, and Africa (or Russia or China) would become democratic. We have seen, however, that democracy is not so easily achieved. Even the United States passed through the collapse of the Articles of Confederation, a disastrous civil war, and a civil rights revolution during its two-century-long quest for democracy. There are still arguments about how close the United States has come to its ideal. Clearly, then, democracy will not simply "come" to Africa in a workshop or textbook or even through a revolution. It must evolve—or be evolved—purposefully. By way of illustration, probably the best long-term African example of democracy is Botswana which can boast of ethnic homogeneity, relative wealth, and educated leadership. A tentative example would be South Africa in 1994 and 1999.

BOX 2.6

TABLE 2.3 (CONTINUED)
Important Dates in African History

1960 CE—Sixteen French colonies attain independence.

1963 CE—The Organization of African Unity is founded.

1960s CE—The Cold War dominates both Eastern and Western foreign policies vis-à-vis Africa.

1970s CE—Drought devastates the Sahel.

1980s CE—AIDS pandemic strikes.

circa 1990 CE—Wave of **democracy** sweeps over Africa. Breakdown of state in Liberia, Sierra Leone, Zaire. Genocide in Rwanda.

1994 CE—Majority rule is achieved in South Africa.

1997 CE—The CIA-supported regime of Mobutu is overthrown in Zaire.

---

*More than twelve million slaves were taken by Europeans, and about four million died in raids or during passage. Africans themselves had slaves, but these were viewed as war booty, temporary servants who could eventually be reclaimed by their own people or released. The slave trade prevented opening of the African interior, dispersed populations, and destroyed some tribes. After the slave trade ended, Africans still kept slaves to produce certain goods and provide services.

†Good Hope refers to the hope of reaching India.

‡Hochschild observes that by the middle of the nineteenth century, the long years of enmity, suspicion, violence, and double-dealing had produced an atmosphere of bitter hostility between African and European traders (see chapter 4.)

lated should be listened to. For example, when a **state** (e.g., Kenya) has a population growth rate of 3 percent and half its citizens are under the age of 15, there are simply too many people. They tax the carrying capacity of the country. Rudimentary eco-

---

STATE

Countries are conventionally referred to as states in political science. A state in the U.S. political usage would be termed a province.

BOX 2.7

---

nomics makes that clear. Unless there are great natural resources (such as in a Persian Gulf oil kingdom), there must be a favorable balance between those who produce wealth and those who consume it, and with a rapidly growing population, that balance is disturbed. While very young children can be made economically productive after a fashion, the greater accumulation of human capital comes from training those children in school so they can

INDEPENDENCE

This term denotes a political condition: freedom from external control. Thus, for example, France is independent, or autonomous. However, there are limits to this condition—i.e., France is constrained by its membership in the European Union, by treaties and arrangements with other countries, by the finiteness of its resources and policies, by the action of other "independent" entities which exert influence, and by natural disasters.

The smaller a state's resource endowment in all senses of that term, the less able it is to exercise independence. A poor African state—e.g., Sierra Leone—may be independent in a technical or legalistic sense, but in actuality it is subject to the whims of its neighbors, the actions of the great powers, forces in the international political and economic systems, natural phenomena, and the malfeasance of its enemies. So independence is a qualified condition for most states, especially in Africa.

The independence acquired by most African states in the 1960s and 1970s had enhanced value for two reasons: It engendered the euphoria that accompanied the ability to act for oneself in the international arena after a hundred years of colonialism. And reciprocally, the international system, especially the United Nations, eagerly welcomed the new states, enhancing their impact beyond their innate capacity to affect that system. (See also *sovereignty*.)

BOX 2.8

contribute more significantly at an older age. Unfortunately, the exponential population explosion in much of Africa has confounded attempts to achieve this. Perhaps if the AIDS epidemic is as widespread as some data indicate, population growth will be severely affected, with a perversely salutary effect on the development of human capital. Of course, there are better ways to accomplish this.

The rapid urbanization resulting from population migrations, not economic development, which occurred in the early days of **independence** has declined somewhat. Distressing urban slums (as seen in South African townships or Nairobi, for example) have perhaps deterred some who might otherwise have moved into cities. Unfortunately, since in many places the population explosion has made it impossible for everyone who wants to have access to land to have some, it is not feasible simply to espouse a rural resettlement program, and slums remain, fostering disease, crime, and social decay.[5]

There are many reasons for declines in agricultural production: Periodically, drought descends on many regions of Africa, making reliance upon farm income unreliable if not impossible. For years, food in cities was subsidized since that is where the power structure is located and where a revolution is most likely to be fomented. This practice, however, so minimized income for farmers that many farmers were induced (or forced) to seek other sources of income, thus forgoing surplus production for sale in the cities. **Structural adjustment** programs implemented by the International Monetary Fund require real market prices for basic commodities, which further disrupted markets, though theoretically it should induce farmers back into food production by guaranteeing them a fair return. Just because there is a crop does not mean there is a market; not all agricultural production can be readily converted into income, and not all agricultural production is conveniently processed or stored. Extensive overplanting, lack of crop rotation, planting on marginal soils, and employing less than effective tilling techniques[6] have caused agricultural production to drop in recent years. Finally, few African farmers have access to modern technology. Much human labor is involved in farming with few animals and only an occasional tractor, but production is low on a per capita basis. These factors keep many people tied to the land at subsistence levels, and few are able to con-

---

STRUCTURAL ADJUSTMENT

Specifically this is an expectation imposed by the International Monetary Fund. It requires debtor states to adjust their financial structures to bring them more in line with the Western model—internally and externally open markets, unsubsidized production, market pricing that reflects real production costs, and other factors that minimize government interference in the market.

Generally, structural adjustment plans include the following features:

- devalued currency to encourage exports and discourage imports,
- efforts to balance the government budget by cutting expenses,
- movement to a free market economy by ending government subsidies on some products,
- markets open to free trade,
- privatization of state-controlled business, and
- increase in interest rates to encourage savings (instead of consumption).

Whatever the merits of such plans, they have created substantial economic disruption where they have been abruptly imposed—e.g., when the subsidized price of basic foodstuffs rose precipitously to reflect "real" costs. Zambia and Tunisia suffered demonstrably after structural adjustment was imposed.

BOX 2.9

---

vert agriculture into large-scale wealth or food surpluses. Food supplies—or the funds to purchase food in the international marketplace—are so marginal that many African countries have suffered major famines since 1950.

NOTES

1. In case there is still someone who has not heard it: Several blind men encountered an elephant for the first time. Since they could not see it, they had to use their hands to gain an impression of what an elephant is like. Afterward, they were asked to describe it. The one who had grabbed the elephant's leg averred that an elephant was like a tree. The man who had gripped the tail countered that it was like a rope. And so on. All were correct to a degree, and none was entirely correct. It all depended on the perspective.

2. This topic will be revisited, but for the moment it suffices that roughly the northern half of Sudan belongs to the Maghreb in its culture, religion, history, and politics, while the southern half belongs to Africa for similar reasons. As of this writing, however, Sudan, at least politically, is one, and it is included in our Africa.

3. Both the tsetse fly and the malarial mosquito are very sensitive to altitude, so cattle thrive on the Zomba Plateau in Malawi, one thousand meters above the surrounding tsetse-infested plains.

4. By thinking of Africa as an upturned saucer, you can understand the difficulty of navigating its rivers. There is a significant rise in elevation relatively few kilometers from the coast around the southern two-thirds of the continent. Once that is traversed, however, riverine navigation is widely possible.

5. I recall the pineapple vendor who frequently visited our door in Nairobi. Thinking that I knew best, I asked him why he did not return to his village rather than suffer the miseries of a marginal existence in a very crowded, unhealthy, and unfriendly city. He explained that he had several older brothers and his father's land was insufficient to provide acreage for all of them, so he was forced off the land. When I pressed him on why he did not buy some land, he explained that tea plantations in his home region had driven up the price to US$4,000 per hectare, a fortune to a man who peddles pineapples at 25 cents apiece.

6. One caustic observer suggests that Malawi's number one export is topsoil.

The Colonial Experience: Precursor to Subservience

Contact with Europeans transformed Africa and Africans in ways that are at once profound, complex, obvious, and difficult to comprehend. Remember the Jahn quotation at the beginning of this book: "[T]he Africans are for the most part ignored." The African was in many ways made a stranger in his own land. There is a wry but accurate comment about South Africa: When the Dutch came, they had the *Bible*, and the

The Western world continues to "colonize" Africa. Note the sign for Gilbey's (British) Gin [far left], Volvo (Swedish) cars [upper right], and of course the bus carrying the visiting Chicago Bulls.

Africans had the land. After a few years, the Africans had the *Bible*, and the Dutch had the land (see Michener).

For many years while I assimilated what I knew and thought about Africa, I resisted making relative cultural assessments. I adhered to the "politically correct" dictum that **cultures** were undoubtedly different, but none was inherently better than any other. However, that is simply not true. Think about this: Which is better, a fork or a spoon? Of course, the logical response is, in assessing a culture, *What will you use it for? What is its purpose?* If one is eating soup, then a spoon is clearly better. But if one is cutting meat, then a fork (and a knife) is preferable. So, What purposes does one impute to culture? Does it foster development? What is essential to survival? How significant is dominance by another culture? Is happiness integral to development considerations? How does one define progress? And what do these terms mean in any given context? As with questions of utensils, one

CULTURE

At the risk of practicing anthropology without a license, I define culture as the cumulative practices and beliefs of a fairly homogeneous group. Cultures evolve over time in response to environmental change. The purpose of this evolution is survival, adaptation to changes which may be gradual or revolutionary, progressive or regressive. The "evolved" culture may be more or less adapted to a subsequent environment, and if it is too maladapted may disappear. The meeting of Africa and Europe precipitated a period of rapid and far-reaching cultural conflict and evolution, primarily for Africa. Not all was salutary, nor was all bad; most was somewhere in between. One must approach the study of Africa with an acceptance of this cultural continuum.

BOX 3.1

notion is not inherently better. Each is suited to a purpose; that is how they evolved. But if one is fed only a diet of thin soup, the spoon may be essential to survival.

CULTURE AND COLONIZATION

Ali Mazrui a preeminent spokesman for contemporary Africa, imputes to "culture" several specific functions, among them perception, motivation, stratification, communication, and identity (p. 47 ff.). His view of motivation is pertinent to this discussion in that he sets out four levels of needs in traditional African societies:

1. individual basic needs,
2. the basic needs of the wider family,
3. the need for individual advancement, and
4. the need to promote the welfare of the larger family (59).

This mix of community and individuality sets Africa apart from the individualistic tradition of the Greco-Roman, Judeo-Christian West which generally emphasizes (1) and (3) over (2) and (4).

ALI MAZRUI

Ali Mazrui is the preeminent African political scientist. After training at Makerere University, he later returned to teach. The regime of Idi Amin purged the university of most scholars, and Mazrui exiled himself to the United States where he is presently on the faculty at the State University of New York at Binghamton.

BIOBOX 3.1

European (colonial) culture evolved in a temperate climate, over a long period of conflict and contact, and it developed to maximize certain values which are traceable to Greece, Rome, and early Israel. Diamond argues that Western cultures also evolved as they have partly because great latitudes of similar climates provided for easy expansion over territory, creating large empires and reducing internal conflict. African cultures (and there are perhaps a thousand) evolved in greater isolation from one another as well as from outsiders and on generally smaller scales. Their climate is primarily tropical, and their value system supports different objectives.

Depending on how we measure contact, we could say that these cultural traditions—European and African—have interacted for a hundred to five hundred years. However, whenever they have met, the Europeans have clearly triumphed—at least in terms of European values. The Europeans control the land; they have subjugated the African economically, socially, and militarily virtually wherever they have confronted one another. So the Europeans are better at "winning" on their terms. And their terms have dominated global interactions since the Middle Ages. An expression of dissatisfaction with African tradition is reflected in an article on the "gender" page of *The Nation* (Blantyre) in February 1997. Citing the plight of a recent widow whose relatives insisted that she wear black for two planting seasons and stay confined for a month after her husband's burial, the reporter cites property grabbing as the relatives' motive.[1] She advocates fighting such "oppressive customs."

During African-European interactions, other important events were taking place outside, and beyond the control of, Africa—major developments of modern society such as transportation, weapons, communications, and medicine. While the African walked, the technologically more advanced Westerner arrived in a four-wheel-drive truck or an airplane. While the African relied on a snare or arrow to bring down an enemy, the European employed bombers, ships, and missiles. While Africans distributed information quite effectively for their purposes through the "jungle radio"—orally or occasionally with drums—Westerners blanketed the continent with radio waves in various languages. Different circumstances, different purposes.

Jared Diamond argues that Europeans surpassed Africans technologically because of their greater variety of edible plants and domesticatable animals. These enabled the Europeans to establish settled societies and thus to develop technology, which gave them the advantage in dealing with Africans.

Living symbiotically with nature, unlike the West, Africans are more aligned with natural forces than are residents of the industrial West. If there is no electricity, one rises and retires with the sun—there is no need for a clock. If the seasons are fairly constant, there will be maize or cassava or rice tomorrow just as there was yesterday, so there is little incentive for developing elaborate food processing and storage technologies. If the group is more significant than the individual, social institutions evolve based on communal values which are entirely different from the individualistic Western values manifested in capitalism, post-Reformation theology, and Greco-Roman conceptions of the individual. In an American divorce court, these would be termed "irreconcilable differences."

The Europeans came to Africa, however, not to meld cultures, not to match values, not to exist symbiotically with Africans. Europeans came in pursuit of wealth, power, prestige, markets, raw materials, land, and occasionally on spiritual missions. Power took the form of military posts, personnel, slaves, trade, fulfilment of manifest destiny, and protection of existing wealth—all of which produced a spiral of increasing needs for European settlers and an increasingly complex maze of cultural interactions for Africans.

Prestige meant many things to Europeans, but the more area a state could colonize, the better. This was reflected in the British epigram, "The sun never sets on the British Empire" (which once included, for example, St. Lucia in the Caribbean, over fifteen African colonies including Basutoland in southern

Africa, Ceylon in south Asia, and myriad other marginal locales). The presumed wealth which colonies produced (gold, ivory, slaves) equated to prestige and power in Europe. Finally, great power status was conferred simply by holding colonies (hence Germany's insistence upon the Berlin Conference[2]). The Berlin Congress was a mechanism for heading off intra-European conflict over the search for colonies which had become a **zero-sum**

ZERO-SUM

This concept from game theory describes a game designed so that winners and losers are equally distant from a mutually-desired midpoint, and one participant cannot win unless another loses. Other games are "some sum"—i.e., all or some participants may "win," as when the first three runners to cross a finish line gain, respectively, five, three, and one points.

Whether an activity is zero-sum or some-sum is determined in the mind of the player: If I perceive your action as hostile to my interests—regardless of what you intend—and you succeed, then I will lose, at least psychologically. If you do not define your action vis-à-vis me as competitive, you may regard the very same activity as some-sum or neutral.

African states have cast a very wary eye upon the international political system while at the same time large powers have acted with impunity to seek their objectives regardless of what Africans wished. Consequently, one side's perceptions did not reflect those of the other side. This has often left the Africans feeling exploited, while Western states especially have puzzled at the lack of gratitude for their assistance. Example: During the Cold War the United States and the Soviet Union competed vigorously for influence in Africa. When an African state sided with one power, the other power saw that action as a loss, regardless of its intrinsic significance.

BOX 3.2

---

race for influence. This implied competition among aspiring European powers to best their enemies, past, present, or future. If France had much, England needed more and better, and so on. As they sought to expand their empires, the French and British converged upon Khartoum in Sudan where the British prevailed, depriving the French of their chance to control an East-West route across the continent, and raising British hopes for a railway from the Cape of Good Hope to Cairo (a dream that was never realized).

The idea of colonial markets was generally oversold, but it appealed to an industrializing Europe which was moving rapidly into surplus production for which it had no existing markets. Gandhi's epic battle against British mercantilist policies reflected this.[3] In many locales, trading companies were granted monopolies—e.g., the British East Africa, the German East Africa, the British South African Chartered, and the Royal Niger Companies; the Association Internationale du Congo and the Compania de Mozambique. Clearly, the Europeans had great expectations.

These expectations were unrealistic. The commercial presence required military protection at a substantial cost to the imperial power. As postmodern colonialism (i.e., current European-African economic relations) demonstrates, one can develop economic relationships and advantages without the costs of colonizing. Britain's economic dominance in most of her former African colonies obtains here. That the Japanese have cornered the automobile market in much of Africa is even more revealing. Consider two of the less successful colonizers. Less than one percent of Italy's trade was with her colonies between 1894 and 1932; instead, the colonies actually *cost* one billion lire more than they returned in trade. For Germany, the story was similar: From 1894 to 1913, only .4 percent of her trade was carried on with her colonies.

Another supposed benefit of colonization was the gaining of an outlet for surplus or disruptive populations. This did not prove effective either. In thirty years, only twenty thousand Germans migrated to colonies. In the sixty years following 1865, thousands more Dutch returned to Holland than migrated to her colonies (though none was in Africa). Ninety percent of Europe's emigrants between 1886 and 1936 selected the New World, not Africa, for settlement. While the Portuguese had some success in inducing citizens at the bottom of the socioeconomic ladder to accept land in their colonies, the numbers were not sufficient to prevent the 1974 **revolution** that brought down Portugal's dictatorship and its subsequent loss of colonies.

Trade is a two-way exchange, so it is not expedited by the selling of slaves. Slaves were not significant to trade because they were stolen, and there was no reciprocal accumulation of resources with which to purchase production from the metropole, much less from other locations. Concomitantly, plantation agriculture was introduced, and it served the purpose of providing needed raw materials to metropoles. It also induced residents of colonies into the money economy: they worked not at food production for their own consumption, but at producing, for exam-

---

REVOLUTION

As opposed to evolution, revolution is an abrupt, irregular change in a system, often associated with an ideology. Revolutions have taken place regularly in Africa, most of them relatively bloodless because of the lack of weapons available to most people. Only a small number of "revolutionaries," generally the military, were armed, suggesting that some measure of broad support favored the change. The Ethiopian government's overthrow by Mengistu Haile Mariam was a revolution—as was his subsequent overthrow some years later. One of the most "relaxed" revolutions occurred in Zaire/Congo in 1997.

BOX 3.3

---

ple, groundnuts for export. As tea, groundnuts, or cotton production was expanded, greater and greater economic control was exercised by the colonial institutions. The more people entered the money economy, the more detached they became from traditional, conventional village life.

Trade was further inhibited by the imposition of taxes in many colonies. This, too, succeeded in driving the inhabitants into the money economy, but the tax was collected to support the colonial presence, not to provide services or infrastructure to residents of the colonies. Its effect, therefore, was to remove some available resources from the general economy. This entire process never made the colonies profitable.

The economic disruption that followed the introduction of colonial practices was very much akin to problems of economic development in other times and places. Chief among these were:

1. Urbanization with its attendant problems of crime, crowding, disease, technological revolution, unemployment, and social disruption;

2. Disruption of food production as farmers were forced from, or induced off, their land and into the money economy, to work in services or mining, and to pay taxes or become consumers;

3. Productive land appropriation for plantation agriculture (export crops such as sugar, cotton, groundnuts, tea), reducing food production and forcing the remaining farmers to find less productive land, leading eventually to deforestation, erosion, and desertification; and

4. Family disruption as breadwinners (almost always men) were drawn into paying jobs in distant cities or mines.

In numerous instances, humanitarian interventions, have been conducted by **missionaries**. Missionaries were not an unmixed blessing, but it was their agitation in Europe that put an end to slavery. Medical services, education, and technology flowed from a variety of sources. Of the first round of African heads of state in the 1960s, the great majority were educated, at least in part, in schools established by missionaries. Missionaries, however, often came with the intention of "picking up the white man's burden."[4] The Belgians reified this attitude in their motto applied to the Congo: *Dominer pour servir* (To rule in order to serve).

In *Things Fall Apart*, Chinua Achebe wrote of the profound social cleavage created by missionaries in his home country. Competition between sects, unwillingness to permit Africans to

---

MISSIONARIES

Readers are invited to think beyond the superficial when considering this term. There is a widespread inclination to give the benefit of the doubt to people who serve humanity as missionaries. Much good undoubtedly has been done by missionary activity— e.g., schools, hospitals, and churches have been built, and technical assistance has been provided. But there is also a very real and pervasive downside effectively presented by the Nigerian author Chinua Achebe in *Things Fall Apart*.

First, one must decide what to think about the bringing of religion to the "heathen." It is not difficult to imagine the cultural imperialism conveyed in the expectation that you, the missionary, have something to teach me that is preferable to what I have been taught all my life. Implicitly, I have been wrong and you are right. Also, a certain divisiveness may be more or less overt in missionary activity. What the "true believer" accepts is correct, and what the unaccepting infidels espouse is wrong, or even demonic.

Even when such sentiments are not explicitly articulated, they constitute an undercurrent in any missionary activity. Indeed, much intolerance has been advocated in the name of religion.

BOX 3.4

---

move upward in church or educational hierarchies, and the attraction the church held for society's least successful made the missionary presence less than a blessing. Missionaries, in short, were a mixed bag—some generous and accepting, others patronizing and rigid. They did some good, created some problems, and altered Africa's history for better and for worse.

Just as it is difficult to generalize about Africa itself, it is misleading to generalize about the colonizers. The colonial administrative techniques adopted by the four major powers (Britain, France, Belgium, and Portugal) differed markedly, however similar their outcomes.

The British ruled indirectly, a technique developed around 1900 by Lord Lugard, the Governor of Nigeria. Having overextended his control, he was forced to rely upon thirty-eight local authorities to exercise his writ. This technique proved very effective. It required minimal British presence and expense and it only mildly disturbed local life. The British presence in any colony was reinforced by the Anglican church and its parallel administrative structure, though it did not actively proselytize.[5] The British administrator at the primary level was the District Officer who exercised a broad spectrum of authority and was required to learn the indigenous language and to collaborate with established authorities.[6] The British, as well as the other powers, always assumed they had sufficient time to bring to fruition any grand plans for their colonies before independence would be seriously considered.

In the process of their indirect rule, the British strengthened and supported traditional authorities because they expected British standards of order and behavior to be willingly enforced and emulated. Eventually, self-government would evolve. Large colonies were equipped with universities, several of which became quite distinguished—e.g., Makere College in Uganda. In the last decade of the empire, the 1950s, the British provided US$1 billion in development funds to enhance infrastructure in their colonies.

France operated at the other end of the spectrum: Her rule was direct and "idealistic (or unrealistic)"; Africans were expected, in effect, to become "black Frenchmen," learning the language and embracing French culture and practices. Traditional rule was ignored, replaced by French law and custom, including government ownership of all land not individually owned. Civil servants were sought on the basis of **meritocratic** standards from a class—*evoluées*—who spoke French, were Catholic, and had a French education. This process of direct rule required four times as many administrators as Britain's indirect rule. In a departure from the general French detachment from ongoing activity in their colonies, following World War II all French colonials were given citizenship and parliamentary representation. It is a measure of their meager infrastructure that only a very small French expatriate community remained following independence. France did not push for wide-

MERITOCRATIC

Ever since the Renaissance, the Western world has operated implicitly on meritocractic principles. That, is we do not hire your brother for this job *because* he is your brother; he may be hired, but only if he displays the qualifications necessary for the position. This assumption that skills and job requisites are related and measurable is a clear example of Newtonian cause and effect.

The alternative is some form of preferential hiring based upon family, tribe, relationship, bribe, or whatever. Access to a position is gained either on an objective basis or on the basis of preference (or sometimes on a combination of the two). In a preferential system, one cannot expect predictable, high-quality outcomes. The striving toward a modern political and economic system is, in effect, a striving toward a meritocracy.

BOX 3.5

spread education; in fact, in 1957 no more than 10 percent of school-age children were in school. The characterization generally applied to the French colonial policy was paternalism.

Belgian rule was rooted in the curious beginning of the Congo as a colony. It was administered for a decade as the personal possession of King Leopold. His "colonial policy," consisted of extensive and aggressive exploitation. The Governor of the Congo observed at one point, "Self-government is no substitute for good government." The Belgians did not ever consider local self-rule. The only residents who enjoyed rights were the equivalents of French *evoluées*. Prior to independence, higher education was available only through the church and for the church; as a matter of fact, at the time of independence there were no more than fifteen university graduates in the entire Congo—all of them priests. Still, half the school-age children were in primary school in 1957. This Belgian administration has been described as "platonic" in the sense that its guiding principles were far removed from reality, envisioning an ideal situation. People were not prepared for a future different from the specific present. As a result of this lack of training for the indigenous population, the Congo—though more densely administered than any other colony—produced a less prepared citizenry when independence finally arrived.

The Portuguese were forced to surrender their colonies in 1975 after protracted civil wars on the African continent and a revolution at home. They had offered rights only to *assimilados* (those who accepted Portuguese common law, were self-supporting, had no tribal contacts, and read and spoke Portuguese). These amounted to less than 1 percent of the population at independence after three hundred years of Portuguese administration. In 1950 there were only 737 African primary school students in these colonies. In order to bring inhabitants of the colonies into the money economy, residents were compelled to engage in contract labor on Portuguese-owned plantations. Once an indigenous African became assimilated, however, racial antipathy did not exist—at least until the last few years before independence. At that time, poor Portuguese were granted land in the colonies in a futile attempt to head off civil unrest at home. To lower their colonial "profile," the Portuguese proclaimed the colonies "ultramarine" provinces of the homeland; they displaced local governments and avoided reporting to the United Nations on "non-self-governing" territories. The revolution in Portugal was in substantial part a consequence of the unacceptable cost of repressing dissent in the colonies, leading to a new level of enlightenment and a hasty end to their empire, many times larger in area than Portugal itself.

The Germans and Italians had brief colonial episodes, the Germans losing their four locations—Togo, South West Africa, Tanganyika, and Kamerun—in the Treaty of Versailles which concluded World War I. Libya was awarded to Italy when the Ottoman Empire collapsed in 1911, and it occupied Ethiopia by force from 1933 till the end of World War II.

Policy analysis includes evaluation of costs as well as benefits in assessing the wisdom or correctness of the policy. While colonialism was not a policy *of* the colonies, it was a policy with profound impact *on* them. Whatever may have been its effects (costs and benefits, real or perceived) on the imperial powers, there were clear costs and benefits for the colonies themselves. We turn now to an examination of this balance sheet.

Obviously, some benefits accrued to colonies as a consequence of the colonial experience, but benefits and costs are value concepts. Although we are writing from hindsight and from a Western perspective, we have tried to maintain academic dispassion and objectivity.

There were, let us say, four benefits of colonialism: stability, economic **development** (technology transfer), the introduction of Western civilization, and humanitarian exchanges. Each of these can be debated, but on balance it appears that Africans generally have persisted in their desire to acquire and appropriate these values into their own systems and lives. Therefore, they must perceive them as generally beneficial. It is difficult to argue, for example, that better health as a result of smallpox inoculations

DEVELOPMENT

This is a political as well as an economic term. It is *assumed* by many that it is the normal human condition to develop, that tomorrow will be better than today. Whether history confirms this epistemological notion or not is arguable. Furthermore, it is subject to individual interpretation. Do we define development as simply having a roof over one's head, a suit of clothes, and access to the World Health Organization's daily minimum calorie intake? Does development mean having a satellite dish, an automobile, a refrigerator, indoor plumbing, a computer, etc.? Or is development a matter of free speech, freedom of religion, and access to a liberal education? Until we know where we are going, we cannot select the route we will travel—or recognize the place when we arrive.

BOX 3.6

W.E.B. DUBOIS

W.E.B. DuBois was a leader of the African diaspora—those many peoples in the Americas and Europe who had roots in Africa. As a writer and scholar, he popularized the notion of negritude, the cultural wholeness of the Black peoples. Not surprisingly, he was a persistent critic of Western governments and systems, so much so that he moved to the Soviet Union after its revolution and propagated communism until his death in 1940.

BIOBOX 3.2

is anything other than a benefit. Likewise, the establishment of a university is almost universally seen as a good, but not everything that emanates from its halls is uniformly good: What about the cultural depreciation that occurs when students are forced to become, in effect, English or French and forgo their own culture?

The American Pan-Africanist W.E.B DuBois observed that in the West the century between the Congress of Vienna in 1815 and the outbreak of World War I in 1914 was seen as a century of peace. This was a very Eurocentric view because that was also the century of colonial expansion in Africa—which was anything but peaceful from the African perspective. Once the colonial enterprise was settled by the Berlin Conference, there was stability in most of Africa, a welcome change from slave-taking and colonial competition, but still an era of massive human rights violations, particularly in the Belgian Congo.

FALLOUT FROM COLONIZATION

Economic transformation of their society resulted when Africans were brought into the money economy—not on their terms. Was this advancement? Or simply material movement? Setting aside epistemological issues, the global popularity of, for example, bicycles, television, and medicine—which one associates largely with Western societies—suggests at least that the Africans have more of what *they have learned to want* as a consequence of the colonial experience. And they continue to desire more and more. This desire for more motivates the garden boy who is slashing grass in the yard of the house where I am writing this. He works a twelve-hour day for about US$35 per month. Otherwise, he has the option, at least theoretically, of returning to a rural subsistence existence devoid of economic development and Western technology. He epitomizes Elspeth Huxley's observation: "Who are we to tell them to work harder when we make a principle of doing less ourselves?"

Aside from theological issues of "salvation," etc., it is clear that there were beneficial humanitarian exchanges during the colonial period. The cultural disruption so effectively chronicled by Achebe goes on the "cost" side of the ledger. Teachers, physicians, veterinarians, translators, and others with humanitarian instincts were sent by religious groups. Nelson Mandela described the exchange this way: "Yet even with the [colonialist attitudes of missionary schools], I believe their benefits outweighed their disadvantages" (p. 53). On several occasions I have spent time at the Mennonite Guest House in Nairobi. It is frequented by present-day missionaries, and I am regularly surprised by the wide array of talents they display,[7] not to mention their commitment. Clearly many are making significant contributions.

Sociologists employ the term anomie to describe a sense of depersonalization, of being deprived of a sense of identity. As a consequence of several processes—e.g., forced labor, contract labor across boundaries, migration to urban areas in search of employment or education, religious proselytizing, or cultural dominance—many Africans have ceased to be themselves and have, in effect, become someone else. These changes, which many people in all cultures experience to some extent have been more difficult for Africans to accept because they have in large part been imposed, not adopted voluntarily. In contrast, the experience of a university education produces change, more in some people than others, but that change is voluntary. People enter upon the process of higher education with the expectation of and desire for change, but the changes colonialism brought were not ones for which people volunteered nor which they had any voice in determining. Nor did all the requisite social and material tools with which to deal effectively with colonialism accompany the arrival of new values and priorities.

The final phase of social replacement is, in effect, the complete destruction of the old society. That does not necessarily imply that a new (improved or inferior) society will arise in its place, only that old conventions—those customs that have evolved to govern human behavior over time—will erode. Ad hoc rules of behavior may be the response of many, especially those living at the margins in a very different milieu from that to which they were accustomed. This does not lend itself to a stable society, development, progress, or a sense of community.

English and French are the dominant languages throughout urban, educated Africa. One observer says that the colonial experience made the "African a stranger in his own land." Traditional values no longer create the environment that pervades a given locality. Western (taken broadly) values are more likely to predominate in a complex combination or to have completely replaced traditional ones. As urban areas grow and peoples from different backgrounds mix, traditional values are submerged, and the dominant replacement value is that of the colonial experience. For example, though there are many ethnic groups in Kenya or Tanzania, the operative language is English—not simply because it is legally imposed, but because it is functionally required. The same is true of French in Senegal. The language of international commerce, of tourism, of academia, of research is functionally English for much of the world. An individual may elect not to learn English in Kenya, but that choice assures the individual of economic marginalization.[8]

More significantly, change does not occur selectively. One can be taught habits of hygiene, but those will not answer the need to purchase soap for washing hands, for example, or the need for a privy—which implies the need for a shovel. One thing leads to another. One cannot have a bus system without clocks, wrenches, and petroleum. Small changes, thus, have far-reaching implications. For example, the hygiene lesson may be nearly cost-free, but the soap may be manufactured by a British or U.S. firm, so the benefit is double-edged: health for the hand-washer means profit for the manufacturer and a negative impact on the country's balance of payments. Clearly, not all of these were the teacher's intention. And while the message may be hygiene, the learner may be more profoundly impressed by the messengers' style of dress, treatment of colleagues, or drinking habits than by any information about germs, so there may be other outcomes than the expected result.

The societies established by the Europeans in Africa were for their own benefit only. If Africans wanted to participate at any level, they had to do so on European terms. Mazrui argues that Europe affected only sociopolitical conditions, not such other arenas of life as the ecological or technical (p. 7). This is seen in styles of dress, forms of housing, language, etc. The direction of change came from outside Africa. The Europeans wanted a railroad built here and a mine there, and the Africans had to adapt to those developments. Furthermore, the taxes imposed by Europeans forced Africans to work for wages and leave their settled or

---

REVOLUTION OF RISING EXPECTATIONS

Before you knew about Nintendo, were you unhappy that you did not have one? Of course not; you cannot dwell on what you do not know about. So it is with developing areas. Being exposed to the modern world—whatever its manifestation: television, Nintendo, health care, bicycles—raises people's expectations and foments desires for things they now know about but do not have.

This process can be exacerbated by demagogoic leaders who promise much more than any political system can deliver . An otherwise conservative leader, Nelson Mandela promised millions of new housing units to his population, which was as much as one-quarter homeless. Not surprisingly, such units could not be delivered as promptly as had been promised, which gave rise to disappointment and potential political unrest. Whether such expectations engender revolution remains to be seen.

BOX 3.7

traditional lifestyles, regardless of their wishes. This prevented any spread of the "free rider" syndrome. It was "pay-as-you-go" paternalism: to benefit from the colonial system, one had to pay, whether one accepted the benefits or desired them or not. The Africans were compelled, in effect, to participate in the destruction of their own cultures as they labored within the infrastructure of colonialism.

Once the process of change is let loose, no resources will satisfy the cravings that are created. If a few people have bicycles, refrigerators, and educations, most people will desire them. This produces a **revolution of rising expectations**. One's desires arise as a consequence of awareness (of bicycles, for example), and unfulfilled desires lead to revolutions of various sorts. The US$1 billion in **development assistance** provided by the British to their colonies in the late days of colonialism could not begin to bring everyone to the level of the economic elite, though all had growing aspirations. Given present resources anywhere, the civilities of modern living cannot be brought to everyone.

Akin to the revolution of rising expectations is the fact that change is an ongoing process, and it may go slowly. It will not be sufficient to have hospitals and schools only in the capital city or to have automobiles or televisions for only a select few. Everyone will want to participate in the good things of economic development, so the change must continue indefinitely. We have certainly witnessed that in the West. This is the underpinning of economic development and commercial success on the one hand; but on the other hand, it can lead to addiction to the culture of materialism.

Much as a rigid religious education (e.g., Amish, Muslim, or Catholic) is designed to insulate the young from alien ideas, so the colonial experience served to insulate colonial peoples from a variety of experiences. The Portuguese colonies were submerged in their own culture and education. There was no British or Peruvian or Polish presence. Compare this to the United States during the same period when peoples of myriad nationalities and backgrounds

---

DEVELOPMENT ASSISTANCE

In the days before political correctness, the term was foreign aid. The phrase simply means resources which are transferred from external sources into a system for its use. The ostensible purpose of the assistance is to further development, but definitions of development may differ markedly, so the outcome is uncertain. My favorite example is the well-meaning American who installed a bathtub at a wellhead in East Africa for cattle watering. So far, so good. But in order not to waste precious water by having the well flow continuously and the tub overflow, he installed a float-type valve (such as is found in toilet tanks) to turn off the inflow when the tub filled. Just think about such a mechanism—which does not last all that long in the security of a toilet tank—in an environment of dirt and grime, being nudged by thirsty cattle and subjected to tinkering by preliterate cattle herders. Could this be viewed as development?

Development assistance also has a political aspect. Rich country A wants to influence poor country B so it provides whatever it values—maybe a mainframe computer, maybe a four-lane highway. The cost is high, the intent is benevolent—but what good is the computer if there are few trained technicians? Or the highway if few people have automobiles?

BOX 3.8

---

emigrated, bringing with them matzos, jazz, St. Patrick's Day, and much more to contribute to an enriched, synthetic culture.

In the colonies, a new **oligarchy** with new values was created. Partly because of the need to train a cadre of civil servants for indirect rule in British areas and partly to implement imperial policy in other areas, education and training were provided—selectively. Those who received it were much advantaged compared to their peers, and over time many moved skilfully and successfully into positions of substantial power and prestige. While some of the origins of this process were in the meritocratic filling of positions, it was soon perverted to favor sycophants, the devious, "true believers," and others far removed from conventional channels of authority or administration. The learned skills contributed to preparing people for the "brain drain" by which highly educated and talented people extracted themselves from their home environments and moved profitably into Western societies.

Most European economies, especially as they benefited from colonial empires, were much more nearly autarchic than the very small economies of Africa could ever aspire to be. In economic terms, autarchy is the ability of a state to be economically independent, not dependent on others for the essentials of devel-

---

OLIGARCHY

From some political perspectives, it could be argued that an oligarchy exists in every state—an elite group which controls the financial power and, consequently, the decision making. Certainly, most African states at one time or another have been oligarchies. For example, the Emperor and his extended family constituted an oligarchy in prerevolutionary (1972) Ethiopia. In a very different way, the entire English population constituted a kind of oligarchy in premajoritarian South Africa where they dominated several layers of the population: Blacks, Asians, Coloureds, and also Afrikaaner whites. If one accepts this as an inevitable consequence of contemporary economic life, then the question becomes not whether there is an oligarchy, but *who constitutes* the oligarchy at a specific time and place. In many African states this question is not difficult to answer with a few day's observations or a few well-formulated questions. The next question is: Is the oligarchy benign or malevolent? Many African states qualify today as oligarchies, e.g., Kenya, Malawi, Mali.

BOX 3.9

---

opment and progress. In the 1980s the GNPs of at least fifteen African states were smaller than the sales income of the 500th largest global business.[9] Britain or France with their millions of people and varied resources could easily conceive of producing books or electric mixers or tennis racquets; the same expectation would be fanciful for a place like Togo or Swaziland. Consequently, small or nascent economies continue to be held hostage by colonial relationships whether they want books, electric mixers, or tennis racquets. Over time these relationships become ever more complex and intentional, especially on the part of imperial interests.

From a larger political perspective, observers—regardless of their value perspectives—find empirical consequences of colonialism. Africa has over fifty states with average populations of ten to fifteen million. Not only are these nations small in population, they are generally small in area, particularly in terms of arable or useful land and resouces. So only a few African states—most notably Nigeria, South Africa, and Zaire[10]—can reasonalby aspire to any significant international position.

In a postindependence reaction to colonialism, Africans took an interest in things non-Western—particularly socialism-communism in the economic realm, unipartyism in the political realm, and Islam in the religio-cultural realm. During the Cold War, African states (joining such others as India, Yugoslavia, and Indonesia) chose, for the most part, to be "nonaligned"—independent of both the United States and the Soviet Union. This choice was a reaction against the importuning of the superpowers. If states readily fell into one camp or the other, there was little need to induce them to that side. The great bribes went to the undecided or wavering (the construction by the Soviet Union of the Aswan Dam in Egypt is an example).[11] African states for philosophical, political, and/or self-interest reasons refused to be cast as pawns. They particularly resented the West, where lay the roots of colonialism.

A certain tension had arisen among the European powers

when they saw uneven empires developing in the early 1900s. The Germans and Italians especially were unhappy with their relatively small holdings. While there were many other factors which contributed to the two World Wars, their disappointment with the outcome of the race for colonies did nothing to ingratiate the other European powers to them.

The data suggest that small colonies performed somewhat better than larger ones. These differences, of course, may be due to nothing more than the small sample size and the particular members of the sample. It is apparent, however, that both British and French colonies performed much better than either Belgian or Portuguese, and the colonial systems are clearly responsible for these differences.

If one reduces the economic calculation to GNP growth, then by examining 1971 data a few years after independence for most colonies, one finds little difference among the several categories of colonies, at least on the three scales employed in table 3.1. This may or may not prove anything; it does at least indicate no great disparities and suggests that variables other than the colonial experience account for any differences.

This chapter is entitled "Precursor to Subservience" because the colonial period, despite some clear and unarguable benefits to Africans, was also an unfortunate experience which has resulted in the subservience that is the predominant political and economic fact about Africa today. To wish it away would be neurotic, if not psychotic. Empirically, one must see that Africa today is a bewildered and largely unhappy place.

For example, in the last years of President Nelson Mandela's regime in South Africa, there were rumblings of dissatisfaction. His coming to power was perhaps the most widely heralded political event in several decades, but there were unfortunate concomitants of his rise which linger and may tarnish his political legacy. One was the popular expectation that emerges when the enemy is finally undone and a hero comes to power: now surely things will get better. When some promises of Mandela's—e.g.,

TABLE 3.1
Data Comparing Different Colonies 1969, 1995*

	1969			1995			
	1 *Average GNP per capita*	*2* *Population Growth Rate*	*3* *GNP Growth Rate*	*4* *Average GNP per capita*	*5* *Population Growth Rate*	*6* *GNP Growth Rate*	*7†* *Change*
British							
Large	$130	2.7%	0.7%	$310	2.6	2.8	145
Small	$100	1.9%	2.3	$923	2.3	3.4	297
French							
Large	$223	2.5%	0.6	$630	2.6	1.6	118
Small	$ 84	2.5%	0.1	$272	2.7	2.1	744
Portuguese	$185	1.3%	2.7	$247	2.5	2.9	44

*Large British colonies: Ghana, Kenya, and Nigeria. Small British colonies: Botswana, Gambia, Malawi, and Sierra Leone. Large French colonies: Algeria, Cote d'Ivoire, and Senegal. Small French colonies: Benin, Burkina Faso, Mali, Niger, Togo. Portuguese colonies: Angola, Guinea-Bissau, and Mozambique. Belgian colonies: Burundi, Rwanda, and Zaire.

†Column 7 is calculated by averaging the three average changes between the 1969 data and the 1995 data: i.e, there was a 138 percent change in large British colonies' GNP, a 4 percent drop in population growth rate change, and a 300 percent increase in GNP growth rate. The average of these three is 145 percent—the number in column 7.

housing for all—could not be fulfilled promptly given known resource constraints, there was political unhappiness in large sectors of the population.

One cannot read Fanon, Plato, Jefferson, Christian writers, Thiong'o, or Marx and not see that there is an alternative to the constrained existence for those who must live under even enlightened colonial rule. The paradox of an educated elite caught up with the imperial powers. The inevitable political direction of Western ideas, especially those transmitted in higher education, was a desire for independence. The colonizers needed an educated cadre to manage the colonies, but in the process of transmitting that education, they were transmitting the seeds of the undoing of their colonial system. For example, if this is a meritocratic process, why do whites win every competition? If this is the rule of law, why are some given the benefit of a legal process and others jailed—or worse—with no recourse?

Despite revolutions and political rhetoric, unfulfilled expectations remain. As tourists, businesspeople, or political visitors walk the streets of African cities, they inadvertently exude affluence. Their clothes, their electronic gadgets (watches, video cameras), the food they demand with their dollars, the style of life they take for granted in European hotels—all these contribute to a sense of alienation, anomie, and frustration for Africans. Many of them see no way to achieve decent living conditions, much less real affluence. Are they better off with occasional access to medical care or a modicum of education if they only circle the table—even prepare it or clear it off—but never sit down to the feast?

Place yourself in the shoes of an African: His/her life expectancy may be 45 years, depending on several variables.[12] Life has gotten perceptibly worse for most. Overcrowding, political disorder, AIDS, a declining standard of living, and natural disasters have plagued the past generation. Many of these obstacles arose from, or were worsened by, the colonial experience. Would not the "average" African be as well off if the colonial experience could be rolled back and history replayed?[13]

That cannot happen, of course. We eschewed neurotic

behavior a while back, and we must do it again. But it is instructive in understanding Africa to think about the consequences of the colonial experience for most Africans in terms of whether they have actually benefited or not. The answer is neither unambiguous nor particularly clear.

NOTES

1. Du Chisiza, the preeminent Malawian playwright, produced "Barefoot in the Heart" satirizing this pervasive practice.

2. The boundaries created at the conference were largely artificial, ignoring both natural features and logical cultural divisions. One observer determined that 44 percent of boundaries followed parallels and meridians, 30 percent were simply lines or curves on a map, and only 26 percent had topographic underpinnings.

3. During India's preindependence era, Mahatma Gandhi assiduously spun cotton and wove plain cloth in defiance of British textile manufacturing which transferred value to British textile mills and deprived Indians of jobs.

4. The title of Rudyard Kipling's paean to colonialism, "The White Man's Burden."

5. In Moslem areas, British missionaries were permitted to enter only with the agreement of local authorities.

6. The institution of the District Commissioner (or Area Commissioner in some places) persists to this day. In at least one former British colony, it is extra-constitutional and not subject to legal challenge.

7. My favorite example is an engineer who had developed a fence to keep hippopotami out. Since they lift their feet only slightly as they shuffle along, he placed in the ground staggered rows of posts a few inches tall. He was at work on a giraffe fence at the time we talked! His wife's interesting project was investigating natural nutrition and medications for camels, a herd of which she had purchased and was managing.

8. This has implications for language competence and dominance beyond Africa.

9. Michael Kidron and Ronald Segal, *The New State of the World Atlas*, New York: Simon & Schuster, 1984, #30.

10. As this is written, Zaire has undergone a political transformation, the outcome of which is unclear. Its *nom du jour* is Democratic Republic of the Congo.

11. The Aswan Dam has proven a mixed blessing: It has made irrigation possible in southern and central Egypt, but its flawed Soviet design is causing Lake Aswan to silt up, rendering the dam decreasingly useful.

12. According to the U.S. Bureau of the Census, life expectancy in Malawi by the year 2010 will be 29.6 years, a direct result of the AIDS pandemic.

13. There is no cry for the return of colonialism, in either Ethiopia or Malawi, but many people in both locations would advocate the return of their previous autocratic regimes under the leadership of Emperor Haile Selassie and Life President Kumuzu Banda, respectively. These autocrats served them better that the "democratic" systems that are now in place. In the eyes of those who must scramble day to day to survive, political openness is not, ipso facto, an improvement. Economic circumstances impinge upon people nonstop while opportunities to exercise political liberties arise relatively seldom; so there is often less enthusiasm for political change than for economic change.

CHAPTER 4

Postindependence Africa

It is possible to characterize postindependence Africa with generalizations keeping in mind that there are exceptions to each of them. First, from a superficial political perspective, Africans have clung to their colonial divisions with a vengeance even though many, if not most, are incorrect. That is, these boundaries do not delineate a recognizable

Street vendors in Mafeking, South Africa have set up informal trading outside a department store. The vendor in the center is selling day-old chicks. The word "Bombay" painted on the store window suggests that it might be owned by Asians, who comprise a substantial portion of South Africa's mercantile class.

geographic, cultural, or historical situation (see chapter 3, foot-note 2). Yet Africans have generally agreed that any changes would require other revisions which would impose unacceptable costs or produce relatively few benefits. So in this sense at least, Africa has been exceedingly stable.

At independence, the initial problem confronting the typical African state was the need to establish its authority and allow it to claim **legitimacy**, both internally and externally. The internal

LEGITIMACY

This is the characteristic a system or a leader must have—or be believed to have—in order to be taken seriously and even in order to survive. The level of tolerance in the system is reflected in the eagerness of support or the level of dissent which occurs after a change of regime. Legitimacy can be accomplished in various ways: If there is a recognized process of political selection—e.g., regular elections—that process can confer legitimacy. In most African states there is no such tradition, and governments have come into power largely behind loaded guns. Once established, such a regime can gain legitimacy, even if it is repressive or venal, as long as widespread acquiescence exists.

Where perception of legitimacy fades or disappears, civil disobedience of various sorts is likely to arise—e.g., nonpayment of taxes, off-the-books economic transactions, guerrilla activity, verbal rebukes, and the like. The nexus of a system and its critics determines which carries the day. Normally the existing regime prevails, but history has demonstrated that many systemic changes can be chalked up to loss of legitimacy. **Example:** The current president of Zambia came to power in 1991 in an election that was described as "free and fair," though some contended that it was rigged. Which of these assertions one believes affects one's perception of Chiluba's legitimacy.

BOX 4.1

challenge was threefold: First, the new state had to transfer sovereign allegiance from the generally unpopular colonial regime to that of the new independent government, a task not readily accomplished. Government was not viewed as inherently legitimate, but rather as an enemy from the days of colonial misdeeds and preindependence clashes. The preceding regime was often resisted, even by force.

Second, the challenge to deliver expected services on the basis of very limited resources remained. While the colonial powers promised little and felt less obligation to respond to political expectations, the new governments inherited expectations that were constantly rising, exacerbated by political rhetoric. But the new governments did not have access to the resources of the metropole, and external assistance has never been remotely adequate for responding to demonstrable, much less political, needs.

Third, governments had to deal with multiple ethnicities. In some states (Mali, Botswana) this problem was inconsequential, but in others (Sudan, Nigeria) it persists as *the* political problem. The possibility of providing incentives or establishing order as a means of achieving allegiance was restricted by limited resources. Compelling loyalty was an option, but it could spark a dangerous reaction. Zimbabwe, with an 80 percent-20 percent ethnic division between the Shona and Ndebele, arrived at a dominance-subservience relationship comparatively easily. Ethiopia, on the other hand, is coping to this day with traditional domination by the Amharas who constitute less than a majority of the total population.

The unified front which emerged from resistance to colonial authority eroded in the face of the Cold War, natural disasters, and economic trials. The absence of a common and visible enemy, colonialism, substantially raised the cost and lowered the likelihood of coherent action. This situation is not unlike the difficult restructuring of alignments in post-Cold War Europe.

Military intervention—whether internal, from a neighboring state, or from the metropole—was a possibility in most states.

In times of deprivation, the military in most African states is often the best-equipped element, receiving several times more in budget allocations than ministries of health or education (see table 5.4). Theoretically, this should assure the status quo; a few guns will carry the day against no guns at all. Since most states sought to establish a military capability to ensure the survival of the regime (if not for international adventures), militaries grew powerful. Global military spending is roughly equivalent to the combined annual income of the poorest half of the world's population. Put differently, the income of the poorest half of the world could be doubled if there were no military spending by any states. For example, in 1991 Ethiopia and Mozambique both spent the equivalent of more than 10 percent of their GNPs on the military. In another manifestation of imperialism, the largest suppliers of weapons to developing states are the world's major powers (the permanent members of the U.N. Security Council, to be precise), and arms sales create a technological, if not political, dependency.

POLITICAL STRUCTURES

Institutions of modern government in colonial Africa—to the extent that they existed at all—fulfilled the purposes of the colonial powers: to extract raw materials and taxes, to manage the population, to stave off neighboring intruders, and to produce crops for export. Governments did not exist primarily to benefit the citizenry. Since colonial regimes had been perceived as exploitative—some, such as the Belgians in the Congo, in the extreme—there was overt resistance to government in all its manifestations. Further, since the colonial regimes had served only colonial purposes, there was little interest in assuring that the writ of the central authority extended equally effectively to all corners of the territory. Some areas were essentially ungoverned in any conventional Western sense. The new governments had to introduce and enforce governance on the inhabitants of these areas.

The indirect rule that characterized British and to some extent Portuguese and Belgian colonialism further eroded the potential of central institutions. To this day, traditional rule exists side by side with Westminster-style institutions in many locations, reflecting the fact that it is easier to "join them" than to "fight them."[1] Several examples of frustrated centralization can be seen in Zaire, Ethiopia, and Sudan.

African geography played a part in determining the level of governance in different regions. For example, the savannahs with their more hostile environment required more complex decision-making procedures. Kinder environments elsewhere presented fewer challenges and consequently required less government. Areas with very sparse population (i.e., deserts) had little governance. Government was also less apparent than in Western societies because of material shortages. For example, practices such as licensing businesses or maintaining standards of hygiene in food production were irrelevant to much of Africa. Government is irrelevant, so government is less apparent and more distant.

The shortage of a trained cadre of civil servants contributed to **uniparty** rationales and was also an impediment to establishing the legitimacy of government. There were so many

UNIPARTY

This self-explanatory term denotes a political system that is not *multi*party, a system in which a single party dominates. In such situations, political competition can occur only in the context of the party—that is, in a manner similar to the Democratic or Republican primary contests in the United States. The term is nonjudgmental: the single party may be sinister—as in Stalin's Soviet Union or Mengistu's Ethiopia—or benign—as in Nyerere's Tanzania.

BOX 4.2

tasks to be performed and so few qualified people to perform them that governments had to rely upon one of three options: employ unqualified civil servants, retain expatriates who had served in a given capacity prior to independence—and were therefore reminiscent, regardless of their individual behaviors—of colonialism, or leave posts unfilled and the tasks undone. A combination of all three techniques was usually employed. For example, until the late 1980s the chief executive of the University of Malawi, an institution created at the time of independence, was an expatriate. Europeans still fill cabinet posts in several African states.

The form of governance that emerged in most newly-independent states and which prevails in many today is the uniparty system, characterized by a party and state which are effectively merged. Nyerere's Tanzania was a classic example. Uniparty systems generally had the following characteristics:

- All-inclusive; no other political participation was permitted or recognized
- Parallel or identical party and political structures
- Charismatic leadership, often originating in the anti-colonial struggle
- Confinement of opposition—if any—to intraparty competition; no competing political structures
- Conservation of scarce human resources; talents were put to work where they could be most productive
- Preclusion of class divisions—at least in theory; no elite, no economic oligarchy, and no ethnic distinctions
- Self-perpetuating political oligarchy

Underlying uniparty development was a form of anti-Westernism. Former metropoles, for example, exported replicas of Westminster's parliament (right down to the powdered wigs) to Africa. This was silly, incongruous, irrelevant, and defiant of local preferences and traditions. Uniparty systems were seen as an authentic African substitute.

POWER ELITE

This term, coined by the American sociologist C. Wright Mills, refers to that small segment of any society which is in effective control of the distribution of major resources. In a typical African system, its members might include some or all of the following: primary members of the central government, members of the legislature, upper-level police and army officers, significant expatriate and national business owners, prominent clergy, media owners, and their family members.

BOX 4.3

Uniparty systems were easily susceptible to manipulation by the elite. With access to the limited media sources in new states, those who were media savvy could overwhelm those who were not. And because an elite controlled the political structure, it was natural for external interests to connect with that elite in hopes of acquiring future business opportunities. It exemplified the oft-repeated axiom: *The rich got richer, and the poor got poorer.*

Not unique to Africa, but more influential when constituted authority is less effective, are elements of the civil society that operate outside government. Fatton explains that this situation "privileges the privileged and marginalizes the marginalized" (p. 72). Those who "knew the ropes" were those whose hands were on the ropes; they constituted the **power elite** and were able to turn the operation of the system to their advantage—often permanently.

The expectation—entertained especially in the United States—that democracy would characterize the new political systems in Africa was inherently unrealistic, reflecting ignorance of or inattention to the African "situation." Democracy is not a system of governance; it is a cultural phenomenon, a condition cultivated over a period of time and evolving slowly from tradition as it gains legitimacy. The Africans had no experience in managing a modern nation-state, and most of their states were multiethnic, not "nation"-states. Democracy depends upon several foundational elements: tolerance of loss and of victory for the other side, an informed electorate[2], and a willingness to abide by rules. Fatton suggests the "institutionalization of uncertainty within a predictable framework within which outcomes are neither permanent nor arbitrary" (p. 87). In the colonial period (1890–1960), this was not the way government operated. In traditional Africa, different political processes also prevail.

In those few cases where democratic or reasonably **participatory** regimes did come into power, they remained fragile and often fell prey to military coups. Nigeria has gone through several power transformations, but democracy has not yet been sustained for more than a few years at a time. In late 1995, twenty-

---

PARTICIPATORY

A better description of some governments than "democratic" would be "participatory." This term suggests less about structure and more about process, indicating that the citizens of a state participate in some legitimized manner in choosing policies and politicians. It does not imply any particular structure and does not necessarily suggest majoritarianism. A uniparty system such as Nyerere's in Tanzania in its early days could be participatory even though it lacked some standard hallmarks of Western democracy. The question then becomes, "Is the given system more or less participatory?" **Example:** The 1994 and 1999 South African elections were authentically participatory.

BOX 4.4

TABLE 4.1
African Trade as a Proportion of Global Trade

US$billion	1989	1992	1995
World	$2,965.5	3,726.3	$5,031
Africa	64.3 (2.2%)	82.2 (2.2%)	96.6 (1.92%)
Industrial States	2,119.3 (71.5%)	2,602.1 (69.8%)	3,233 (64.3%)
Western Hemisphere (excluding U.S. and Canada)	114.4 (3.86%)	182.8 (4.86%)	247.2 (4.9%)

Source: Data from *IMF Balance of Payments Statistics*, 1996.

five African systems were in some phase of democracy (according to the Carter Center which follows and facilitates movement in that direction. See table 6.1). Only time can tell whether there will be a similar number of authentically democratic regimes some years from now.[3]

ECONOMIC FACTORS

Let us now turn our attention to economic characteristics of postindependence regimes. Many commentaries on Africa imply that no governance measurable by conventional Western taxonomies existed prior to the coming of the colonial powers or prior to independence. This perception was reinforced by the image of the "dark continent" that filled European literature during the early years of exploration and beyond. In fact African societies had political and economic institutions from time immemorial. Unfortunately for the Africans, their systems were observed and interpreted by the dominant Europeans, and their traditions were not consonant with European ways. In the face of more powerful European systems, they were forced to submit to the dominant paradigms—to which they were permitted to contribute little or nothing.

Where tradition continued, Fatton argues, "[Its] persistent power of tradition paradoxically symbolizes people's logical answers to the uncertainties of bastardized capitalist modernity" (p. 75). There was no full agreement in the West on the appropriate solution to economic organization of the modern industrial state. The excesses of capitalism, the original modern Western economic mode, gave rise to socialism and communism in Europe, and many early African leaders were well-schooled in those excesses—having been the victims of colonialism. Furthermore, African tradition was essentially socialist-communal in economic organization, so it was not surprising to find variations in "African socialism" as it was implemented in several African states.

That tradition also flies in the face of the core of capitalism: self-interest. African practices of ownership constituted a "mixed" economy: Land was communal, but animals and homes were generally individually owned. If the human propensities that flaw capitalism had been managed so as to counter the inherent flaws in socialism, the Africans might have been onto something.

Explanations of the failures of socialism are well-rehearsed in the West, and they have been confirmed historically—with a few exceptions—by the collapse of socialist systems in all corners of the globe. This does not mean, as one U.S. writer argued,[4] that history has ended and that every critic of capitalism has capitulated. It is unarguable that capitalist states have demonstrated impressive capacities to harness resources and produce awesome quantities of consumer goods, but they have not been as successful in terms of other values—e.g., providing the good things of the system equitably to all its members or incorporating traditional practices into a modern society. These are issues of importance in Africa. Further, when unrestrained capitalists exploited their respective systems to victimize Africans, their exploitation became indefensible.

When traditional economies confronted the global economy that was emerging about the time of Africa's wave of independence, the difference in scale was enormous. As larger systems sought to organize smaller ones, the flow of resources overwhelmed many traditional systems. Leaders who were the gatekeepers for access to local wealth found that position to be a hitherto untapped source of wealth. For example, by requiring an "access fee" under whatever guise, political leaders could become economic players at the expense of multinational business.

In one mode of exploitation, multinational businesses were legitimized by taking on local partners. These businesses were eager to coopt members of the local elite to "front" for them, and they rewarded their local partners far in excess of the value their services would have on the open market. Over time, this largesse became an expectation, and international business did not enter a market without going through the proper political-bureaucratic channels, creating a cottage industry that made millionaires of many African leaders.[5]

Gaining control of a state's economy was difficult under any circumstances because of the diffuse nature of economic activity in Africa. Much of it is inherently "underground," in the form of informal transactions between street vendors and customers, barter in villages, cash payments for ad hoc services, and so on. It was impossible for a government to gain enough control to tax or even to estimate the size of economic transactions. In the 1980s it was estimated that two-thirds of Uganda's economy was off the record; for the Central African Republic, the estimate was three-quarters. Consider many of the transactions one engages in routinely in Africa: purchasing fruit, fish, or vegetables from vendors at one's doorstep or in a streetside market; or purchasing chairs (or even paintings or sculpture) from a similar source. How can this be taxed?

Since Africa's economies were, to use Wallerstein's term, peripheral to the core states of the industrial West, control—in every sense of that term—was exercised elsewhere, and the Africans had the choice of going along or losing out. If a commodity was important (valuable or rare), the Africans themselves were often only marginally involved. The Belgian interests that control the copper and cobalt mines in southeastern Zaire, for example, supported rebels in an effort to gain a controlling interest in the seceding polity as well as in the economy of the state that might have emerged if Shaba Province had seceded from Zaire.

The role of women is pertinent in more than economic matters, but the economic data are so striking that I include some of them here. In the 1970s the United Nations published findings on the nature of women's work. Women had distinctly different roles from men, worked much harder, and were responsible for the more important aspects of daily life—particularly the training, if not the educating, of children. Table 4.2 reports the findings of the UNECA in 1975.

TABLE 4.2
Activities of Rural Men and Women in Africa*

Percent of Total Labor in Hours	*Men*	*Women*
Cut down forest, stake out field	95	5
Turn the soil	70	30
Plant	50	50
Hoe, weed	30	70
Harvest	40	60
Transport crops from field to home	20	80
Store crops	20	80
Process crops	10	90
Market (including transport)	40	60
Trim tree crops	90	10
Carry water and fuel	10	90
Care for animals, clean stables	50	50
Hunt	90	10
Care for the young and the aged	5	95

Source: Data from UNECA, *Women of Africa: Today and Tomorrow*. Addis Ababa: UNECA, 1975, p. 6.

*Most paid jobs in Africa are held by men, leaving women to perform essential but uncompensated chores and to sell in local markets.

Measures of women's disadvantage show a remarkable correlation between low levels of human development across the population in societies in which women receive less education and other benefits.[6]

In any system, goals explicitly or implicitly drive policy: infrastructure, education, social services, capital development, and any other discretionary government activity. This is not to suggest that the goals are salutary, beneficial to most citizens, or even progressive, only that policy is not autonomous, but has roots in preferences based on value choices. Each decision made by a policymaker has implications and consequences; those decisions made in the first blush of independence were particularly pivotal because they constituted the policy in that particular arena for that country.

In any state, however, goals are often determined by forces operating outside the control of the state. This is more generally true in states that are weak, new, inexperienced, or uncertain of their way in the world; or in states obsessed with a narrow range of concerns rather than seeking to develop a broad and coherent policy structure. Such was the case with most African states at the time of independence. They were, by definition, new and weak, finding their way with new policy priorities which, if only for domestic political reasons they felt a need to revise. Concomitant with the emergence of African states was the consolidation of global Cold War politics creating an uncertain but intrusive international environment. Finally, it was tempting for many African states to focus unduly on a narrow range of concerns, particularly in foreign policy. This focus had domestic implications as well, advocating anticolonialism, anti-apartheid, and neutralism. While these were reasonable policies, the attention devoted to them absorbed time and energy which could have been devoted to other domestic concerns and which might have paid larger dividends in terms of development.

As the Cold War intruded further into Africa, decisions made by foreign donors influenced how the situation for many states evolved. Logically, the donor states (and, less so, agencies) were pursuing their own interests, not the interests of African recipients.[7] At the same time—and still today—there emerged the "new world order."[8] For good or ill, it consisted of greatly expanded international trade, growing debt in the Third World, declining ideology, rising cultural concerns, extravagant military expenditures, declining—and then increasing—U.N. influence, and other features largely beyond African control.

The Soviet Union and the United States furthered their growth, enticing states to their respective sides of the superpower struggle by providing arms and assistance—thus creating dependencies. France and Britain contributed to their former colonies, for example, with a lingering French military presence and continuing British financial interests. Meanwhile, the Chinese and some others attempted to gain influence through sales and gifts of arms.

The cumulative consequence of the last thirty years of development efforts by African states, assisted by the international community, is that in most states the average African is less well off in material terms than he or she was at independence, although there is certainly a wealthy elite—political leaders who skim large amounts from government accounts and **IGO/NGO**

IGO/NGO

These are shorthand references to international organizations—governmental in the former instance (e.g., the World Bank) and non-governmental in the latter (e.g., churches). Membership in the former is limited to states, and these groups have been pervasive throughout Africa since the first Europeans set foot on the continent. In recent years their concentration on development has meant the difference between schools and no schools, drugs and no drugs, faculty and no faculty for many African institutions.

BOX 4.5

---

personnel who dispense funds into local economies and live in opulent style. The per-capita GNP in most African states has either not increased at all or has risen and subsequently declined. One overriding constant has been massive population growth rates which have offset any per-capita progress, (see table 2.2.) overwhelmed services, and hastened the environmental degradation already inflicted by nature.

Under the centralized economies—indeed, controlled economies—of many states "parastatals," were created: monopolistic businesses **controlled** by the state and not operating on capitalist principles of profit and consumer demand. By definition, these were large operations—e.g., basic food processors, fertilizer factories, transportation systems, and the like. As such, their creation and direction had great impact on the overall direction of the economy. Unfortunately, these were under the direction of mere mortals, and thus subject to human frailties. Ghost employees, fixed prices unresponsive to markets, lackadaisical marketing, political rather than economic objectives driving decision making,

CONTROLLED ECONOMY

Non-Western economic and political principles were widely adopted in Africa in the early postindependence years, resulting in centralized control of many African economies. On paper, this seems like a wise idea: States could apply sparse resources to focused purposes and prevent them from being frittered away on marginally desirable activities. On the negative side, however, *homo economicus* does not in the long run respond enthusiastically to such direction. Self-interest eventually prevails—which sparks open-market economies as well as structural adjustment. **Example:** Ethiopia under Mengistu.

BOX 4.6

and insufficiently integrated planning all plagued these institutions, with several untoward results:

1. They were seldom profit-making; more regularly, they were a drain on the national budget.
2. Surplus employees crippled efficiency, and productivity was minimal.
3. Prices were structured to benefit consumers, not producers, because consumers could affect policies more directly than producers could; thus, the price structure tilted regularly in their favor and over time became a disincentive for producers, and food shortages resulted.
4. Economic decisions reflected not the preferences of the marketplace but the desires of politicians who set the direction for the parastatal.
5. Since there were no profit-loss statements, there was little incentive to expand markets or increase profits; indeed, the slacker the market, the less work was required and capacity was often underutilized.

To compensate for domestic inefficiencies, production regularly turned to export markets with their coherent mechanisms for generating revenue, regardless of the level of equity. As export production expanded, of course, production for domestic consumption declined and basic necessities had to be imported— which consumed much, if not all, of the export earnings—leaving the balance near or below zero.

None of these disappointing consequences is inherent in a parastatal organization. They are, however, inherent in human nature, especially when there is little or no commitment to an overall organizing principle and when people see their work simply as a "job." By the 1980s, the international community, led by the United States and Britain, announced, "We told you so." Insisting that more incentive-based principles had to be implemented, the Western states prevailed upon lenders—particularly the IMF and World Bank—to require structural adjustment of borrowers' economies as a condition of future financing or refinancing. Since many states had no choice but to roll over previous loans or negotiate new ones to meet large budget deficits, the lenders had substantial leverage, and structural adjustment has been implemented in numerous states—sometimes with salutary effects, sometimes not. There has also been political upheaval as prices of basic commodities rose dramatically, increasing hardships for the very poor. The final outcome of these transformations is still to be seen.

The capitalism thus imposed by the global "core" on the African (and Latin American) periphery was not all good news. Aside from the indignity of being forced to recant their espoused ideology, citizens of many African states reacted when food prices abruptly increased to market levels under structural-adjustment-program requirements. Governments were placed in the difficult position of being compelled by donors and lenders to accept terms which, in turn, imposed hardships directly on their own citizens. The salutary consequence of this policy was that it minimized price distortions between markets and fostered comparative advantage. Structural adjustment encouraged reinvigorated agricultural production, but it also tended to be inflationary.

Lenders also tried to induce domestic savings; if there are no savings, there are no funds to enable entrepreneurs to initiate enterprises. However, impoverished people do not have surplus income, and savings must be extracted from funds that would otherwise go to providing necessities. This expectation is not realistic. In order to attract savings in such circumstances, extremely high interest rates would have to be paid, and loans would be unaffordable, particularly for small businesses.

Of course, the profits from lending accrue to the lending agencies, so a considerable proportion of export earnings is regularly consumed in servicing the debt carried by foreign institutions. In sub-Saharan Africa, debt service more than doubled during the decade of the 1980s—more than in any other area during the same period. In 1970 Africa's foreign debt was about US$6 billion; in 1989 it had exploded to US$256 billion, equal to three-and-a-half times its export earnings. On the positive side, some lenders have forgiven debts—e.g., Canada, several European states, the United States conditionally and multilaterally, through the IMF's Heavily Indebted Poor Country Initiative.[9]

One of the rationalizations offered to justify Western investment and involvement in development is the trickle-down concept, which argues that any investment or expenditure produces a salutary trickle down of wealth from the top to the economic bottom. If a luxury hotel is constructed, there are jobs for engineers, electricians, cement layers, and brick carriers. Resources theoretically trickle down from the hotel investors into the pockets of everyone. There is a double catch in the theory, however: Many of the more skilled jobs are contracted within the investor's home country. As skill levels drop, there are so many desperate individuals seeking to fill those positions that the salary scale is very low and in the final analysis very little trickles down. Instead, the predominant share of the wealth is transferred to the West. Once the hotel is operating, its furnishings, food, bever-

TABLE 4.3
African Debt Service, 1996

	Ratio of Debt to GNP	Debt Service as Percent of Exports
Benin	0.7	7.90
Botswana	0.1	5.90
Burkina Faso	4.4	16.50
Burundi	22.5	60.90
Cameroon	4.6	6.40
Ethiopia	12.9	44.40
Congo	5.3	2.00
Mozambique	12.4	36.90
Nigeria	5.8	46.40
South Africa	0.7	11.30
All Africa	2.5	19.00

Source: Data from Africa Policy Information Center, Background Paper 12, December, 1998.

ages, staff uniforms, and other supplies may also be imported from the West. The only income for locals goes to relatively unskilled staff competing in a plentiful labor market.

The primary forces which governed postindependence Africa, then, were these:

- A lack of political legitimacy and tradition leading to an often-oppressive uniparty system
- A preeminent military which regularly became the dominant force
- Indigenous poverty compounded by exploitation by multinational corporations and local parastatals
- Heterogeneity which impeded or prevented the development of a national consciousness
- Anti-Western attitudes stemming from anticolonialism and resistance to heavy-handed manipulation in the context of the Cold War.

In some ways the postindependence era in Africa has passed. The original generation of leaders has passed from the scene, and the successor generation is less animated by anticolonial sentiments and more by desires for economic development. The end of the Cold War has resulted in the withdrawal of Russia from ideological competition in Africa leaving some political systems to the vagaries of a globalized economy with occasional interventions by the United States and other European powers. Still, coherent direction and sustained cooperation are not apparent as Africa confronts a global economy which continues to widen the gap between its poverty and the growing wealth of the industrial West.

NOTES

1. Traditional practices still prevail in most African states in the conduct of routine social business and as means of resolving disputes. A British acquaintance

who farmed for many years in Sudan and Uganda and consulted for a large international organization decided to retire to Malawi. He acquired his two-acre homestead by asking a chief for the land; it could not simply be purchased in a real estate transaction.

Another friend walked twenty kilometers round-trip to his village because he had a "case" against a distant relative who was pilfering potatoes from his field. No fine was levied; the complainant's purpose was to hold the villain up to public scorn. Were the crime to be repeated, the case would be appealed to a chief and then to a magistrate on the other side of the traditional/modern divide.

2. In 1993 Malawi conducted a referendum to decide whether to continue its uniparty system or convert to multipartyism. Symbols were employed—a lantern and a cock—to allow the largely illiterate population to express their preference. The question is: How informed can a voter be if she/he is illiterate? For instance, could the cock symbol be seen as a promise to provide a "chicken in every pot"? An earlier Kenyan election produced problems for the party of the hammock—it was expected to sleep too much!

3. Democracy has more than political consequences. There were reports in one country that employees told employers, "I don't have to do that any more; democracy is here!"

4. Francis Fukuyama, *The End of History and the Last Man*, New York: Avon Books, 1998.

5. Data are speculative, but it is generally agreed that the most successful practitioner of this skill is President Mobutu of Zaire whose wealth was regularly estimated at US$5 billion (coincidentally, equivalent to Zaire's national debt). On one occasion when I met with the president in New York City, I asked the gentleman who was waiting for the subsequent appointment who he was: A vice-president of one of the Big Three automakers, presumably there to solicit more than an order for a single car!

Before he died in 1997, former President Banda of small and poor Malawi was accused of caching US$40 million in Europe. Others alleged to have enriched themselves include Amin of Uganda, the late dictator Abacha of Nigeria, and Bokassa of Central African Republic.

6. Extensive data are found in *Human Development Report*, p. 118.

7. One vivid example of the domestic benefits of development assistance occurred in the United States following the Vietnam War: A coalition of isolationist conservatives and non-interventionist liberals in Congress defeated the administration's proposal for foreign aid. In response, the National Association of Manufacturers complained that it would cost American business dearly if it had to forgo the sale of manufactured goods which were to be sent abroad as a major portion of that foreign aid.

8. In 1991 I gave a seminar on this topic at an East African university. When I finished, a dean responded: "That is all fine except that the situation is not 'new,' not 'worldly,' and not 'orderly.'" From an African perspective, not much was new, the change was not worldwide, and it certainly had not brought

"order" to Africa. This confirms the title of a film the U.S. Department of State circulated some years ago: *Where You Stand Depends on Where You Sit!*

9. "Debt swapping" is a novel development in debt relief seen in Latin America. Since financial obligations reflecting Third World debt held in Western financial institutions often were seen as of little value because of the uncertainty of repayment; stockholders, for example, were anxious to shed them. On the open market they could be sold for only a fraction of their face value; lenders would write the loss off as uncollected debt, making the accountants happy. For example, bank A holds a $100 note from country B. Eager to dispose of the note, it sells the note in the secondary market for $20. Buyer C, by prearrangement, presents the note to the issuing country, B, and receives $100 worth of local currency for domestic investment. Country B can print money to cover the redemption of the note or find other local funds more easily than it could pay in hard currency. C can then use the local currency to build a hotel which will have some positive economic impact on B. This tends to make everyone happy: A eliminates a bad debt and receives $20. B eliminates an overhanging debt more easily than by repaying in dollars. C obtains $100 worth of local currency for $20. And B benefits from an investment.

This was taken a step further in Costa Rica where the debt was sold to a conservation organization which purchased land for a national park.

CHAPTER 5

AFRICAN DEVELOPMENT

Western Civilization

On a great crest of thunder
Cymbals shattering, trumpets cascading
Goldenly over a tide of violins
We surge to the symphony's climax—
A vast vision of ennobled man
And the glorious destiny of the race;
After, halved by spendthrift applause
We return to the necessary wearisome tasks;
The greasy grime of chimneys and ovens
Bother about quotas, orders to increase the num-
      ber of graves.

—Dennis Brutus, November 14, 1972

Thousands of Hutu, including these children in a camp in Tanzania, have fled Tutsi genocide in Rwanda. They are among the eleven million refugees displaced from their homes in African countries.

What do we mean by development? Many thoughtful people believe as Dennis Brutus does, contending that development is not an unmitigated blessing. Setting that question aside for the moment, we will discuss development in at least three arenas: economic, political, and cultural. We will view it as a *process*, a *circumstance*, and also a *goal*. Palmer (p. 7) defines development as a purposeful change that moves toward the attainment of a specific goal. That is, we can describe a society as "developed"—having completed a process—or as "developing"—seeking to move from one condition to another (a goal which it may or may not attain). Hence, we frequently refer to "developed" and "developing" (formerly "underdeveloped") states.[1] The state of being developed is referred to by economists as having reached the point of **take-off**, at which self-sustaining economic activity continues.

Mittelman, however, paints a much more negative picture of development: In his view, development of the West entailed underdevelopment of other parts of the world. "The same forces which generated development in the West engendered underdevelopment in the Third World" (p. 43). While industrialization has proceeded throughout Western Europe and large areas of Asia, these places do not serve as useful models for Africa. There is now a pervasive revolution of rising expectations in developing

---

TAKE-OFF

This term was coined by the economist W. W. Rostow to describe the situation in which an economy is poised to move technologically and/or economically into the modern sector. The conditions for take off include the presence of savings, shifting a substantial portion of the workforce from agricultural to manufacturing production, availability of education, etc. Every economy is presumed to be aiming for this objective.

BOX 5.1

AUTHORITARIAN

This term describes political systems characterized primarily by the exercise of authority. In such systems generally acknowledged human rights or political freedoms are minimized in order to fulfill the desires of those in authority. **Example:** Zaire under the rule of Mobutu Sese Seko was managed at the whim of the President without regard to the well-being of its citizens.

BOX 5.2

---

areas which did not exist at the front edge of industrialization. Asian industrialization occurred under essentially **authoritarian** political conditions.

Confucian culture led Asian workers to see their responsibilities in a different light than was the case for African or Western European workers. Outside resources were more available to Asian economies from overseas Chinese, the United States (in the case of South Korea), and other sources seeking skilled workforces, stable governments, and mercantilist propensities.

Following is an excerpt from "Images of Rural East Africa"[2] by James R. Hooker. In addition to being a tribute to Hooker's insight and prescience, the fact that they are still very apt almost three decades later suggests the absence of development over those years.

> Where water, fertilizers and pesticides are combined—as in Rhodesia's Mazoe valley—the result is an unimaginably lush garden. The majority of rural Africans approach farming with a hoe applied to a few scattered acres that grudgingly yield a year's staple requirements.
>
> Village life is crushingly dull; money is scarce; personal conflict is constant; and people are frequently ill. Villagers feel isolated from the supposed benefits of

government yet under the pressure of administration.

Why villagers do not go mad on the infrequent occasions when politicians do visit them is difficult to say. Ministers and Members of Parliament descend form their helicopter, light plane, Land Rover, or Mercedes Benz and advise the people to work hard in the fields. The advice is both gratuitous and laughable.

Why the man who has no roads, no water, no credit, no market, no accessible advisers, no transport, and no equipment should be told to think big seems curious. Should someone choose to make the trek from Mongu to Lusaka, Karonga to Blantyre, or Binga to Salisbury [Harare], what then? First, one has to find shelter, a virtual impossibility, then locate someone who can give advice about cheap eating houses, the city layout, and the job situation.

[F]ew people are inspired to take part in a parliamentary silliness that for mediocrity of expression, paucity of thought and meanness of spirit may have no equal outside the Soviet bloc. [A]ll three rulers have to live with the vestigial traditional government, regard it as barbarous and inefficient, surround it with restrictions, and try to incorporate it into the mainstream of modern one-party rule. [E]ach country equates criticism with antisocial activity.

In all three states the 1970s will probably be like the 1960s: population will grow at over 3 percent a year, and food production will increase by barely one percent.

Can government in the Anglo-Saxon sense come to Central Africa? Would it make sense there? Is the style of government presently available in that part of the world good? The answers are negative. [P]olitics in Africa come very close to being a zero-sum game. The party is the people, the leader is the party, ergo, the leader is the people. Anyone can ascertain where critics of the people stand.

Zambia, Malawi, and Rhodesia have an unhappy history, an uneasy present, and a problematic future.

ECONOMIC DEVELOPMENT

Many approaches to the topic of development can be grouped under the heading of political economy, reflecting the requisite dual elements of politics and economics for initiating "development." Economic development, defined as a static condition rather than a process, is a condition in which economic activity has moved from predominantly agricultural work to industrial (or perhaps service[3]) work. There is a positive correlation between wealth (gross domestic product per capita) and the role of agriculture in a state's economy. A numerical relationship illustrates the condition of "take-off" as defined by economists. It is essential that over time income from exports and other external sources exceed imports. There must be substantial savings available for investment. Either food production must create a surplus, or food must be readily obtained in exchange for industrial exports. Post-Newtonian education must be widely available, if not universal. These conditions can exist in stages or levels—the United States at the advanced stage or Costa Rica at an earlier stage. There cannot be development, however, unless most of these characteristics are simultaneously present. As a process, economic development is the acquisition of those resources and skills necessary to achieve this condition.

Historically, three models of economic development have prevailed. First was the development that followed the industrial revolution, beginning in the seventeenth century and proceeding to this day. This model prevailed in most of the states of Europe and North America, and in a few other locations to which that revolution was transported—either physically or in the minds of people (e.g., Israel, Japan, Australia). The second model appeared after World War II when some systems gradually or rapidly imported the essentials of development by dint of hard work and external education (e.g., Argentina, Taiwan, Singapore). Other states are still engaged in this process (e.g., Mexico, perhaps Indonesia). The final model arose in states whose population growth has outrun development efforts (e.g., much of Africa), whose resources are so sparse as to preclude development (e.g., Bangladesh), or whose internal disorder has derailed the process (e.g., Liberia, Cambodia, Zaire). Table 5.1 suggests some of the major mineral wealth to be found in Africa as a basis for development.

The internationalization of competition in an integrated global economy often creates exploitative situations. For example, inferior merchandise is often dumped on consumers just entering the marketplace.[4] Unless there is infant industry protection, it is often difficult for a developing economy to move into production because most products (aside from those which are very fragile or very cumbersome, such as eggs or refrigerators) can be competitively produced in an industrial state and exported to the Third World.

If there is incipient promise in the "market" of development assistance, there is also a concern, over **neoimperialism**. This is a consequence of conscious efforts by erstwhile imperial powers to manipulate economic activity in a developing state by cornering markets or dominating sectors. Table 5.2 illustrates the

TABLE 5.1
Mineral Production in Africa

Mineral	African Percent of World Production in 1990s	Major African Producer	Percent of World Production
Bauxite	18%	Guinea	16%
Chromium	44%	South Africa	38%
Cobalt	76%	Zaire	55%
Gold	32%	South Africa	28%
Manganese	32%	South Africa	5%
Phosphates	24%	Morocco	14%
Uranium	20%	Niger	8%

Source: *Africa South of the Sahara 1994*, 23rd ed. London: Europa Publishers, Ltd.

NEOIMPERIALISM

Once the concept of imperialism is established, very little imagination is required to conceive of neoimperialism. For our purposes, this is the condition in which a former metropole or another state seeks, or is thought to seek, an advantage over a former colony. It is more frequently alleged against Western states than against any others. It is a pejorative term implying exploitation and unwarranted dominance or interference. Obviously it does exist; equally obviously the charge can be leveled malevolently or recklessly.

What is important is to learn to identify it when it does appear, and to separate it from the rhetoric generally associated with such charges. When there is putative sovereignty but behind-the-scenes control by foreign powers or institutions, there is evidence of neoimperialism. It can take many forms and guises, but it always comes down to external domination. **Example:** French domination of the central banks in Francophone Africa.

BOX 5.3

TABLE 5.2
Changes in Terms of Trade 1965–1988

Sub-Saharan Africa (average annual percent)	
1965–1973	−8.5
1973–1980	5.0
1980–1985	−2.3
1986	−23.2
1987	3.3
1988	−5.3

Source: World Bank, World Development Report 1989, p. 151.

TERMS OF TRADE

Terms of trade are the relative values of products being traded between economies. For example, one might receive a tractor in exchange for one bale of cotton. Or two bales may be required at another time or place for the same tractor. These two transactions would indicate that the terms of trade had changed. For all traded commodities, there are implicit, if not explicit, terms of trade.

BOX 5.4

---

disadvantageous trade position of sub-Saharan Africa during the period when it became independent. Neoimperialism is introduced through willing collaboration on the parts of the political and economic elites in a developing state. These groups seek to enhance their own well-being by serving as neoimperialist agents and they are well-rewarded for putting a domestic cover on foreign-controlled activity. When there is an opportunity to make money, financial interests are drawn in; and international sources are very much more competitive than local sources. In order to retain control of the local system, legislation is often drafted to circumscribe the extent of foreign control, but this is often done in collaboration with the political elite who become the prime beneficiaries of the foreign investment.

Constraints on development are obvious. An economic system that is not connected to the global system will inhibit, if not prevent, investment. If there are penalties for various types of transactions, resources will flow to those environments where penalties are not imposed. Bribery is one pervasive form of penalty that has been generally expected and usually acceded to, imposing costs at all levels of the development process.

From a broad perspective, natural, human, and technological resources that usually comprise the inputs of economic activity are not readily available in most of Africa. Few states—

apart from some states south of the Congo River—are well-endowed with natural resources. There are also gaps in human resources. Consider education: People unaccustomed to technology are at a disadvantage in a workplace where most workers are familiar with computers, for example.

There are in every society remnants of colonial-period economic institutions. These neoimperialist elements are waiting to enter the marketplace in competition with an established European or Western firm whose resources are infinitely greater. Food processing, hotel chains, automobile manufacturing, banking, and airline maintenance are all areas of employment from which Africans have been largely excluded or in which they have been severely limited by circumstances that are remnants of imperialism. **Terms of trade** have also impeded African development. Access to the things that characterize modern life became increasingly difficult during the era of independence, and Africans have fallen further and further behind in relation to cutting-edge technological societies.[5] Economists use the term **opportunity costs**

OPPORTUNITY COST

Many colleges and universities offer an academic discipline termed "political economy" because those two concepts—politics and economics—are inextricably linked. In the index of this book, the reader can find concepts from both fields which have been employed to provide an appropriately broad understanding of Africa. Opportunity cost is an economic term.

If you are spending an hour with this book, think of other things you might have done with that hour: learned to rollerblade, painted a wall at $8 an hour, developed a computer program at $85 an hour, relaxed at a swimming pool, or whatever. These alternatives are the opportunity costs for reading this book (what a price to pay!).

BOX 5.5

to describe the alternative actions an individual can take at a given time for economic reward. Opportunity costs are generally higher for those without the experience to recognize and weigh all options. For example, in Africa one sees market vendors stacking and restacking their piles of unsold tomatoes, potatoes, or pineapples instead of aggressively seeking new markets or new products. To behave otherwise, however, would contravene cultural norms, and that constitutes a very high cost.

POLITICAL DEVELOPMENT

> Africans had 3 white men to thank for political freedom: Nietzsche for the idea of a master race, Hitler for trying to implement it, and Marx for raising consciousness of the oppressed.
>
> —Taban Lo Liyong

Political development is ideally characterized by stability, a consensual government based upon broad participation and legitimized institutions and processes. In choosing lawmakers, voters should have an authentic choice among individuals and policies. There should be a generally free press, substantial accountability on the part of leaders, and meritocracy in the selection of personnel and products. Human rights, particularly gender equality, should be widely respected, and there should be openness to new ideas, including those that come from other systems. Of course, the change inherent in development may also be a destabilizing force—remember the Iranian revolution of 1979 when a modernizing traditional ruler was deposed in favor of a very traditional system. While political development, by this definition, prevails in few if any states, it is the measure against which polities can be judged.

One dimension of politics flows from externalities—recognition. In the era of African independence, external pressures intruded upon the autonomy of state (or putative state) systems. South Africa's *apartheid* regime (see chapter 9) moved from oligarchy to representative government largely because of outside pressure.[6] Biafra, an aspiring independent state which separated from Nigeria, did not receive external recognition and collapsed under Nigerian pressure.[7] Increasingly, influence over state recognition is wielded by international interests. This may become a standard factor in assessing political development.

When development is underway, several conditions characteristically arise. A process of education begins, often undergirded in Africa by religious institutions, and grows in response to

JULIUS NYERERE

Julius Nyerere, the first president of Tanganyika/Tanzania, dominated a government which meticulously avoided individual exploitation. His rigorous values were much admired, especially by scholars outside Africa, but his "socialism" was opposed by the West (in the midst of the Cold War) and his tenure ended in economic disaster for his country. Among his other accomplishments was translating Shakespeare into Swahili.

Nyerere's system held that only those expenditures which were consistent with "familyhood" (*ujamaa*, in Swahili) should be pursued. He also advocated very modest salaries for government officials (his was $8,000) and prohibited civil servants from being landlords. Nyerere died in 1999, and despite the failure of this system to bring prosperity to Tanzania, he was hailed for his visionary policies.

BIOBOX 5.1

perceived needs. Accompanying improved education is improved health care—e.g., hygiene, birth control, inoculations. Agricultural output increases on a per-hectare basis through use of fertilizer, irrigation, hybrid seeds, erosion control, and crop rotation. As labor is freed from the land, opportunities open up in the manufacturing and service sectors, which employ cheap, unskilled labor. Manufacturing ideally converts local resources into secondary or tertiary products.

The stability created by widely-perceived legitimacy enables individuals to pursue their objectives without undue interference. No state can develop without a global view, an acknowledgment that it is a participant—whether willing or reluctant—in the global economic village. Leisure becomes more prevalent as surplus is produced in several sectors and individual workers or farmers can multiply their incomes to lift them above subsistence level.

There are, however, negative aspects to development, and it is not unarguable that development is everywhere and always preferable to sustaining traditional modes of activity. Perhaps the most pervasive negative consequence of development is social disruption. Changes in education, employment skills, social roles, transportation, health, or whatever can be disruptive (as captured by Achebe). As individuals move from working the land to other economic activities, tradition is replaced by ad hoc value systems which lead to unintended and unexpected consequences.

Individuals who are implementers of change, who are educated into the whys and wherefores of what is underway can be expected to adapt and prosper in a developing system. However, those whose lives are disrupted without a social context or an understanding or awareness may suffer from anomie or alienation. Similarly, rural residents drawn or forced into urban settings will most likely be separated from culture and tradition, find a depreciated culture, find themselves less able to operate in the evolving society, and become unproductive or even resistant to change.

Along with this physical dislocation can come cultural dislocation in the form of alien practices—e.g., cigarette smoking, alcohol abuse, thievery—adopted as a consequence of the dislocation that presents new opportunities but leaves conventional constraints behind. The revolution of rising expectations, discussed elsewhere, is a logical consequence of development. Today there are more "things" to be desired, but the resources to attain those things may be no more plentiful from the perspective of a single individual.

The cultural dimension is ever more significant. We refer to a "work ethic" in the West. When Germany was reunified in 1991, there was a vast gap between the way West Germans and East Germans approached their jobs. It was not educational, genetic, or climatological; it was a consequence of two very disparate political cultures that had evolved in post-World War II Germany. Africans have cultural patterns which evolved in preindustrial societies, and many of the habits preferred in the industrial West are contrary to those habits which Africans have evolved.[8] In a society in which there is little work to be had, labor comes cheap, so instead of labor-saving devices and practices, there is a propensity for labor-intensive work. For example, the bank will not have coin-counting machines; that will be done by hand. Shops will not have cash registers or computers to record transactions; sales will be recorded in multiple copies in order to satisfy and employ accountants. And so on.

Policies which arose from political necessity in early post-independence Africa were inimical to industrialization, though this was not apparent to most observers at the time. For example, centralized planning was rationalized with such arguments as: The state wants to devote the few resources available to those elements of development that are meaningful to creating a better life (schools and clinics) as opposed to frivolities (bars or hotels for tourists). This was the essence of Nyerere's "African socialism" (*ujamaa*) which alienated Tanzania from the West. Nyerere desired to develop a Tanzania based on policies and institutions which directly benefited its populace, a country that was not a haven for primarily external Western investment. In pursuing this, he caught the attention of the Chinese who did provide some assistance, particularly the Tazara Railway.[9]

CULTURAL DEVELOPMENT

But there are other cultural aspects beyond simple efficiency. There are questions of objectives, of detail, of purposefulness, of commitment—all related to economic development in very direct ways, and seen very differently in Africa than in the West. In Africa the absence of technological experience, often coupled with a casual grasp of science, leads people at times to overlook details. Since little visible progress has been recorded in the lifetime of most people and since progress is not regularly related to intentionality, there is a lack of purposefulness that encourages the idleness so pervasive among many residents of African cities. Likewise, an empty busyness may fill highways with walkers headed for no place in particular. They may simply be drawing closer to where a job might be available—though there is no real expectation that one will materialize. All this inspires a fatalistic approach to life—*que será será*.[10] Inadequate health-care services compounded by the AIDS epidemic leave people to die without appropriate medical care despite the scientific potential for cures. Commitment is derived from a sense that one's effort will reap adequate rewards, material as well as psychological; that one will enjoy the fruits of one's labors. But Africans have too often labored mightily without much to show for it.

Table 5.3 is a summary of African ethnic groups. While the data in this table are rough—having been drawn from varied sources, and depending upon the uncertainty of ethnic identification from an anthropological perspective—they demonstrate the overarching ethnic reality of Africa: Most states are highly diverse; only a few states are effectively homogeneous (Botswana, Burundi, Lesotho, Rwanda, Somalia, Zimbabwe). Many ethnic disputes

TABLE 5.3
Ethnicity

Nation	Tribe	Percent	Nation	Tribe	Percent
Angola	Ovimbundu	37	Congo	Kongo	48
	Mbundu	25		Teke	21
	Kongo	13		M'Bouchi	14
	European	1			
			Cote		
Benin	Fon	25	d'Ivoire	Baule	23
	Yoruba	12		Bete	18
	Bariba	12		Mandingo	16
	Goun	11		Agni	15
	Adja	6		Senoufon	11
	Fulani	6		Kru	9
	Aizo	5		Lagoon	4
	Somba	4		Dan	3
	Banba	4			
			Djibouti	Afar	44
Botswana	Tswana	85		Issa (Somali)	30
	Kalanga	7		Isaak, Gadabourse	24
	Bakgalagadi	5			
	Basawra	3	Eritrea	Tigrinya	50
				Tigre	30
Burkina Faso				Afar	4
	Mossi	55		Beni Amer	3
	Peul, Tamajik,			Saho	3
	Bellah	19			
	Gurumsi	9	Ethiopia	Oromo	43
				Amhara & Tigrean	30
Burundi	Hutu	85		Sidama	9
	Tutsi	15		Shankella	6
Cameroon	Northerners	30	Gabon	Fang	34
	Westerners	21		Non-Gabonese	18
Chad	Sara	28	Gambia	Mandingo	43
	Sudanese/Arab	12		Fulani	13
				Wolof	12
CAR	Baya	34		Jola	7
	Banda	27		Serahuli	6
	Mandjia	21		Aku	4
	Sara	10			
	Mboum	4	Ghana	Akan	44
	Mbororo	2		Mole-Dagbani	16
	Aka	1		Ga-Adangbe	8

TABLE 5.3 (CONTINUED)
Ethnicity

Nation	Tribe	Percent	Nation	Tribe	Percent
Ghana (continued)				Americo-Liberians	5
	Ewe	6		Gola	4
	Guan	4		Mandingo	4
	Gurma	4		Kissi	3
				Vai	3
Guinea	Fulani	39		Gbandi	3
	Malinké	28			
	Susu	16	Madagascar	Merina	25
	Kissi	6		Betsimisaraka	14
	Kpelle	5		Betsileo	12
	Peuhl	1		Tsimihety	7
				Sakalava	6
Guinea-Bissau				Antandroy	5
	Balante	29		Antaisaka	5
	Fulani	23			
	Mandyako	14	Malawi	Chewa	35
	Malinke	13		Nyanja	27
	Pepel	9		Lomwe	15
	Dioula	5			
	Susu	5	Mali	Bambara	30
	Felupe	3		Fulani	8
				Malinke	7
Kenya	Kikiyu	21		Songhai	6
	Luhya	14		Senoufo	6
	Luo	11		Touareg	5
	Kalenjin	11		Marka	2
	Kamba	10		Dogon	1
	Kisii	6			
	Meru	5	Mauritania	Maur/black mix	40
	Mijikenda	5		Maur	30
	Turkana	2			
	European	1	Mozambique		
	Asians	1		Makua-Lomwe	38
Lesotho	Basotho	99	Namibia	Ovambo	46
				Damara	7
Liberia	Kpelle	18		Herero	7
	Bassa	13		Kavango	7
	Dan	8		European	5
	Kru	8		Nama	4
	Grebo	7		East Caprivian	3
	Ma	7		Bushmen	3
	Loma	6		Coloured	3
	Krahn	5		Basters	2

TABLE 5.3 (CONTINUED)
Ethnicity

Nation	Tribe	Percent	Nation	Tribe	Percent
Niger	Hausa	55		North Sotho	7
	Djerma-Songhai	23		South Sotho	7
	Tuareg	10		English	6
	Peul (Fula)	9		Asian	3
	Kanouri (Beri Beri)	5		Shangaan	3
				Swazi	2
Nigeria	Hausa	21		Venda	2
	Yoruba	20		South Ndebele	1
	Ibo	18		North Ndebele	1
	Fulani	12			
	Kanuri	4	Sudan	Arab	39
	Ibibio	3		Dinka	11
	Tiv	3		Nuba	9
	Ijaw	2		Nuer	6
				Fur	6
Rwanda	Hutu	90		Nubian	2
	Tutsi	9		Beja	2
Senegal	Wolof	36	Swaziland	Swazi	90
	Fulani	17			
	Serer	17	Tanzania	Sukuma	12
	Toucouleur	9		Nyamwezi	4
	Diola	9		Makonde	4
	Mandingo	9		Haya	4
				Chagga	4
Sierra Leone	Mende	30		Gogo	3
	Temne	21		Ha	3
	Luba	6		Hehe	3
	Kono	3		Nyakusa	3
	Sherbro	2		Nyika	2
	Fulani	2		Luguru	2
	Loko	2		Bena	2
	Susu	2		Turu	2
	Mandinka	1		Sambaa	2
	Kissi	1		Zaramo	2
				Asian	1
Somalia	Somail (Samaal)	85		European	0.1
South			Togo	Ewe	45
Africa	Zulu	19		Moba	7
	Xhosa	18		Kokotoli	7
	Coloured	9			
	Afrikaaner	8	Uganda	Baganda	16
	Tswana	8		Karamojong	12

TABLE 5.3 (CONTINUED)
Ethnicity

Nation	Tribe	Percent	Nation	Tribe	Percent
Uganda (continued)			Zaire	?	
	Iteso	8			
	Basoga	8	Zambia	Bemba	37
	Banynakore	8		Tonga	19
	Bakiga	7		Lunda	12
	Banyaruanda	6		Nyanja	11
	Lango	6		Mambwe	8
	Bagisu	5		Lozi	3
	Acholi	4		European	1
	Lugbara	4			
	Banyoro	3	Zimbabwe	Shona	75
	Batoro	3		Ndebele	18
	European	1		European	1

Source: Various sources. A major source for minorities is *World Directory of Minorities* published by the Minority Rights Group International, London, 1997. These numbers only suggest the diversity or homogeneity of a given state and should not be taken as definitive.

have resulted in horrendous disorder. While ethnic homogeneity has served Botswana well, it has not been sufficient to assure uniform political views or development in the other states.

Diverse states may be of two types: In the case of Tanzania where no group is close to dominant, ethnicity is not a political factor. In contrast, where one group is dominant (the Amharas in Ethiopia, the Kikuyu in Kenya, the Baganda in Uganda), the dominant group often represses competing groups or one or more repressed groups may rebel.

When all these factors are combined and compounded, a society must deal with a large proportion of the population that is ill-suited to participate in the functions of a modern industrial state.

When individuals in capitalist systems engage in commerce, as a general rule they are not interested in the **ethnicity** of

ETHNICITY

Virtually everyone is "someone" in a cultural or ethnic context. Someone born in the United States likely thinks of herself or himself as an "American," whatever that means. English is the primary language spoken here. One might think of oneself as African-American, Middle Western, and Catholic at the same time. There may be a hierarchy of sentiments, first this, and then that.

Most Africans, however, encounter choices in this arena that are of far greater moment than anything the average American experiences. There are hundreds of ethnic groups (tribes, if one is politically incorrect) in Africa, and ascertaining one's "group" is not so easy. Is it determined by something personal and internal—e.g., into which one is born—or is it something that is defined externally by others and reflected in the way they perceive and react to one? There are ethnicities of both kinds. Some of the ethnic differences are deadly: the Zulu in South Africa or the Ibo in Nigeria have threatened and been threatened, respectively, by neighboring groups. Other differences are inconsequential (as in the multiple groups coexisting in Tanzania).

On one scale, we could argue that national boundaries should respect ethnicity—i.e., lines should be "naturally" drawn between peoples so that all of one group are on one side of the national boundary and all of another group are on the other side. Unfortunately, people do not cooperate; they are thoroughly mixed in their living patterns, especially in Africa, because traditional interactions coupled with colonial policies and slaving served to mix people thoroughly. Table 5.3 presents some of the ethnic complexity of Africa. Note especially how a given ethnic group may be located in multiple states—e.g., Fulani in Benin, Guinea, Guinea-Bissau, Mali, and Nigeria. **Example:** The Hutus and Tutsis in Rwanda and Burundi have a murderous relationship, even though their ethnic differences are insignificant.

BOX 5.6

the owner of the business with whom they are dealing. If, however, it is of great importance to some Africans—so important that they refuse to trade with certain "others" or to work alongside them—modern commerce is constrained.[11] This problem surfaced in the United States during World War II when black Americans were incorporated into the workforce on a large scale for the first time. Some white workers resisted, but the useful circumstance of a national threat outweighed extraneous considerations. Likewise, in a developing economy, the only consideration should be the quality of the work, not such irrelevancies as who is related to whom. But such attitudes are difficult to overcome.

Unfortunately, contradictory human impulses operate in matters economic, and policy has to strike an almost magic balance between them in order to maximize material development. On the one hand, there is selfishness: An individual desires a bicycle for himself, and he may work very hard in the expectation that his reward will ultimately be a bicycle. On the other hand, there is the community interest which is very strong in many African societies: This land, these cows, belong to all, and no one's needs or desires should outweigh the general needs and desires of the entire society. Excesses in either direction of human propensity defeat development potential. The man who works too assiduously for a bicycle may impede another man's opportunity to acquire a bicycle ("restrain trade," in the language of U.S. antimonopoly legislation). If a woman takes too seriously the communal nature of possessions, she may decide that someone else should take care of the cows or the land while she relaxes—leaving resources to deteriorate. The first problem is familiar in the industrial West; the second, in socialist states of Europe and Africa. Economic development requires harnessing the selfish instincts (my desire for a bicycle) with societal planning that will further development for the common good (building a railroad). Alternating between these extremes is like the swing of a pendulum. Rarely does the policy pendulum come to rest for long in an appropriate middle. (See the discussion of agricultural subsidies elsewhere for an elaboration of specific conditions.)

FINANCIAL DEVELOPMENT

Financial policies directly affect the circumstances of economic development. For example, if a currency is freely traded or there are no limits on foreign investment, and profits can be readily repatriated, a state's level of control over its economy is less than if there are restrictions on sending of capital out of the country. In conjunction with the centralized planning that often characterized new African states, a wide variety of controls were put in place to minimize neoimperial interference. At the same time, such controls discouraged investment and trade, driving economic activity elsewhere and discouraging local entrepreneurs.[12]

The policies of dominant foreign states have a particular impact upon inferior economies. For example, the debt crisis of the 1970s was a consequence of factors essentially external to Africa, but its impact was felt primarily on that continent (as well as on South America as debt defaults plagued many states). Since African states make up only a small fraction of the international economy, they are proportionally more subject to its vagaries than more powerful economies, and they are virtually impotent to do anything about it (unless they wish to decline to participate at all as Albania did for many years). That option requires effective control of the flow of information so that citizens do not know how deprived they are—which raises new questions, and new problems. Table 5.4 documents the financial choices made by African states.

Some argue that culture is relativistic, and that is one of the two overarching impediments to development (the other being neoimperialism). Some cultural practices are more conducive to development than others, but *different* is not *better*—nor is it *worse*. Development, as understood in the West and as defined at the outset of this section, has cultural requirements. To

TABLE 5.4
Money Talks: Where Do States Spend Their Limited Resources?

State	1 Public Health Expenditure as Percent GDP, 1990	2 Percent of Population not Expected to Survive to age 40	3 Food Imports as Percent of Imports, 1993	4 Education as Percent of Government Expenditure, 1995	5 Defense as Percent of GDP, 1996	6 Debt Service, as Percent of Exports, 1995
Angola	—	38	—	—	6.4	13
Benin	2.8	27	—	3.1	1.4	8
Botswana	—	31	—	9.6	6.7	3
Burkina Faso	7.0	38	—	3.6	2.4	11
Burundi	1.7	37	16	2.8	4.1	28
Cameroon	1	26	—	—	2.4	20
CAR	2.6	35	4	—	2.4	7
Chad	4.7	37	—	2.2	2.7	6
Congo	—	32	—	5.9	1.9	14
Cote d'Ivoire	1.7	32	—	—	0.9	23
Djibouti	—	33	—	—	5.2	—
Eritrea	—	33	—	—	7.5	—
Ethiopia	2.3	34	6	4.7	2.0	14
Gabon	—	26	—	—	2.0	16
Gambia	—	38	—	5.5	3.9	14
Ghana	1.7	23	—	—	1.4	23
Guinea	2.3	38	—	—	1.9	25

Guinea-Bissau	—	42	—	—	2.9	67
Kenya	2.7	27	8	7.4	2.2	26
Lesotho	—	23	—	5.9	5.0	6
Madagascar	1.3	21	11	—	0.8	9
Malawi	2.9	46	—	5.7	1.2	26
Mali	2.8	36	—	2.2	1.8	13
Mozambique	4.4	38	—	—	3.7	35
Namibia	—	26	—	9.4	3.0	—
Niger	3.3	36	—	—	0.9	20
Nigeria	1.2	31	—	—	2.8	12
Senegal	2.3	32	29	3.6	1.7	19
Sierra Leone	1.7	50	—	—	5.9	60
South Africa	3.2	13	6	6.8	1.8	—
Sudan	0.5	27	—	—	4.3	—
Swaziland	—	21	—	8.1	—	—
Tanzania	3.2	31	—	—	2.5	17
Togo	2.5	33	23	5.6	2.5	6
Uganda	1.6	44	—	—	2.4	21
Zaire	0.8	30	—	—	2.8	—
Zambia	2.2	42	—	1.8	1.8	174
Zimbabwe	3.2	34	18	8.5	3.9	—

Sources: *Human Development Report 1998*, UNDP.

summarize, the requirements include attention to detail, global perspective, a desire to acquire, meritocratic rewards, and broad access to resources.

A society characterized by practices that are not conducive to development has three options: (1) It can "change" its culture, a disruptive and expensive process which is nevertheless accomplished constantly. The preeminent example in recent years has been the emergence of the "tiger" economies of Southeast Asia: Singapore, South Korea, Taiwan, and Hong Kong. (2) A society can reject change and all that change implies, holding to traditional standards and values and eschewing the trappings of modernity. Very few societies have opted for this route, but a few—China under Mao, Tanzania under Nyerere, Greenland in recent years, and other places from whom we have heard very little—have attempted it. (3) A society can attempt to repress or reverse change in the face of global progress (e.g., Iran in the 1990s). This prerevolutionary situation cannot hold for long. States are too permeable in these days of pervasive communications and travel—**informal penetration** in the jargon of international relations—for people to remain unaware of change. People across cultures and

---

INFORMAL PENETRATION

This terms helps explain how Africans operate among themselves. In an age of massive electronic communication, easy and extensive travel, and the spreading of images around the globe, no state can keep its borders sacrosanct. (Although it is true that Albania maintained its extraordinary isolation for fifty years under the regime of Enver Hoxha, that was clearly an exceptional case.)

BOX 5.7

STAGNATION

This is an economic concept describing the situation in which an economy fails to keep up with expectations or with neighbors and competitors. There are myriad causes and few cures. Many African economies have stagnated through no fault of their own, because of the global economy, processes over which these economies had little or no control. Stagnation discourages investment, entrepreneurial activity, and local enthusiasm. People in such situations tend to withdraw from the larger system, precipitating a geometric downward spiral.

BOX 5.8

---

across time have regularly opted for "modernization" over **stagnation** when the opportunity was presented.

DEVELOPMENT AND RELIGION

Religion is a paradoxical force. It can serve as an agent of change or of resistance to change. All religions have starting points, but they are regularly reified and begin to resist change, ceasing to be countercultural. At the same time, when different religions come into contact, there is implicit "competition." Adherents of each faith rationalize their continued belief in one "truth" in the face of another. Table 5.5 provides a very rough census of religions in Africa, recognizing that local variations blur the lines between one system and another. This can actually induce change, as history has shown throughout the ages. New religious movements emerge to replace religious traditions that no longer fit social realities. For example, the Dutch Reformed Church in South Africa—with members of all races—held that God intended some races to

TABLE 5.5
Religious Affiliation

State	Percent Christian*	Percent Muslim	Percent Traditional*
Angola	48 Catholic 8 Protestant	—	—
Benin	12 Catholic 3 Protestant	12	65
Botswana	15 African Independent Churches 15 Other	1	50
Burkina Fasso	8 Catholic 2 Other	25	65
Burundi	50 Catholic 13 Other	1	35
Cameroon	35 Catholic 5 Protestant	20	39
CAR	20 Catholic 15 Protestant	5	60
Chad	6	44	40
Congo	20 African Independent Churches 25 Catholic 10 Other	1	50
Cote d'Ivoire	12	23	65
Djibouti	3	94	—
Eritrea	—	90	—
Ethiopia	30 Ethiopian Orthodox Churches <1 Jewish (Falasha)	30	10
Gabon	60	<1	35
Gambia	10 Catholic	85	1
Ghana	43	12	40
Guinea	2	85	10
Guinea-Bissau	5 Catholic	30	60
Kenya	28 <1 Baha'i	6	26
Lesotho	44 Catholic 8 Anglican 29 Other	0	19
Liberia	75 Official	27	—
Madagascar	25 Catholic 25 Protestant	2	47
Malawi	35 (Catholic, Presbyterian)	20	45
Mali	2	70	20

TABLE 5.5
(Continued)

State	Percent Christian*	Percent Muslim	Percent Traditional*
Mauritania	<1	99 Official	—
Mozambique	12	13	60
Namibia	85 (Lutheran, Catholic, etc.)	—	15
Niger	<1	95	5
Nigeria	21 Catholic 21 Other	52	6
Rwanda	38 Catholic 10 Other	1	48
Senegal	5 Catholic	85	10
Sierra Leone	10	40	50
Somalia	—	99 Official	—
South Africa+	80 Dutch Reformed, Methodist, Anglican, African Independent Churches [White Population 3 Jewish]	20 of Asians [80 of Asians are Hindu]	17
Sudan	15 <1 Baha'i 1 Hindu	75 Official 65	10 —
Swaziland	80	—	20
Tanzania	20 Catholic 10 Other	35	35
Togo	17 Catholic 5 Other	10	58
Uganda	33 Catholic 30 Anglican	5	30
Zaire	44 Catholic 10 Protestant	1	45
Zambia	35 Catholic 37 Other	1	27
Zimbabwe	8 Protestant 7 Catholic 7 African Independent Churches	—	40

Sources: *Worldmark Encyclopedia of Nations: Africa,* 7th edition; Europa Publications, *Africa South of the Sahara 1987.*

*"African independent churches" does not denote a single organization; there are many ostensibly Christian churches with local leaders who integrate elements of European Christianity with local traditional practices and beliefs. The dividing line between traditional practices and Christianity is often blurred.

be superior and others to be subordinate. For a number of years the world body of the Reformed Church exerted pressure on the South African Church, but change is slow, and any revision of that belief in racial hierarchy is still rejected by some groups.[13]

Corruption, which is seen in all societies regardless of the level of development, is an impediment to economic progress. It is, in effect, a tax on development because it extracts resources out of the trading cycle for the benefit of a select few who generally apply the resources to activities not contributing to development. Corruption can take the form of police stopping autos to extract a few coins to supplement meagre or nonexistent wages. As in the case of President Mobutu of Zaire, it can take place on a wholesale basis, allowing a political leader to extract a percentage of all profits from a manufacturer doing business in the state. In either case, it does not further development, and if it becomes pervasive in a society, as it is in Nigeria, the resulting reputation discourages further economic activity, whether it be tourism, investment, or assistance.[14]

If political rhetoric is excessive or unrealistic, and if it persists over time, the populace can be induced into a state of disappointment over promises made and not kept. The energy that can theoretically be harnessed in the pursuit of development can be dissipated if people see their goals in perpetual retreat. Leadership can mitigate the disappointment by blaming external forces—e.g., international financial institutions, neighboring states, religious groups, etc.—but that works only so long.[15]

Some historical events, while not reversible, have residual impact on development. One is slavery, which extracted from the continent able-bodied workers in great numbers.[16] Another is the creation of boundaries by Europeans, boundaries which have no relationship to cultural or economic reality on the ground and leave Africa truncated into economically ineffective microstates. Finally, some of the human legacies of colonialism have impeded development: There are Africans who are convinced that they are developmentally inferior to Europeans, and there are Europeans who reciprocate this feeling. Substantial concrete evidence supports this argument and can prompt a fatalistic surrendering to the present situation without striving to make a change.

On another front, there are also international agencies (NGOs, including churches, and IGOs) which have proliferated in Africa since independence, growing by a factor of twenty in some locations. These organizations often operate with the good of the local population in mind, but their agendas are determined in home offices outside the continent. Resources made available may not be directly pertinent to local needs; priorities can be established which do not conform to local interests or priorities; and the cost of maintaining local representatives for myriad organizations consumes vast resources and serves local needs only secondarily. In the eyes of some observers, such organizations are neoimperialist in that control is retained outside Africa and foreign representatives regularly implement the programs. Many such entities have hired locals in an effort to mitigate some of this criticism.

Development is a complex process. It requires fundamental changes and decisions which do not come equally easily or readily to every society. Such decisions must be made *by* people to be affected *for* themselves, not *by* some people *for* other people.

Suggestions regarding the necessary change were pro-

TABLE 5.6
Economic Development Measures

	$100 GNP per capita	$500 GNP per capita
Percent GNP originating in agriculture	50	20
Percent GNP originating in manufacturing	10	20
Electric power consumer per capita annually	40 KWH	550 KWH
Improved roads per 1,000 square miles	25	400
Literacy percentage	20	85
Life expectancy	38	62
Telephones per 1,000	2	240

Source: Allan Mathews, "Resources and Norms in Development Planning," *International Development Review* June, 1967, p. 11ff.

TABLE 5.7
What Are Reasonable Expectations?

	Development Continuum	
	Rudimentary Infrastructure	*International Standards*
Institutions	Inadequate, understaffed, undertrained	Modern, fully staffed, well-trained
Education		
Primary	Large outdoor classes, fees,no books, poorly-trained teachers, focus on boys, ethnic	Trained teachers, adequate buildings, free books, small classes, all welcomed, national
Secondary	Same as above	Same, options
Tertiary	Nonexistent, religious purposes	Adequate facilities, up-to-date curriculum, secular
Food		
Production	Subsistence, few crops, no credit, no hybrids, costly fertilizer, insecticides, etc.	Hybrids, fertilizer, credit, agriculture consultants, markets, transportation, surplus for trading, variety
Consumption	Unvarying, nonnutritious, sporadic	Nutritious, varied, reliable, affordable
Transportation	Unsafe, inadequate, irregular, expensive, poor roads	Safe, frequent, affordable, trains, good roads, options
Health Care **Availability**	Limited, remote	Appropriate, care for all
Health *Education*	Traditional healers proliferate; academic training rudimentary and rare	State of the art equipment and knowledge; generally available only outside the country
Material Culture	Primitive	Participants in global market
Sources	Locally produced, inferior products, often transnational businesses	Competitive commodities available from export and meeting international standards

TABLE 5.7

(Continued)

	Development Continuum	
	Rudimentary Infrastructure	*International Standards*
Entertainment	Traditional	Variety of options, e.g., cinema drama, radio, television
Tourist Facilities		
	Few, very expensive	Appropriate to attractions, variety of grades
Sports Facilities	"Sand lot" quality	Varied, accessible, well-used
Media		
Newspapers	Few expensive, urban, noncompetitive	Many, inexpensive, national, competitive, unfettered
Radio	One national system	Competitive free market
Television	None	International access

posed in 1967 by Matthews. While the actual numbers are no longer relevant, the issues are. He proposed the changes listed in table 5.6 in order to move a country's per-capita GNP from $100 to $500.

Obviously, development is not an absolute condition; it is relative to one's expectations, one's past, one's potential, one's neighbors. There is not an absolute condition of *developedness*. It is more nearly a process consisting of multiple factors than an objective condition. As a normative condition, it is reflective of the societal values of those who are developing. The following matrix suggests the kinds of considerations implicit in evaluating development.

The underlying concept that progress is good must also be considered. Does every African need to be like every Westerner for good to be achieved? Is it even possible? Who can legitimately make such decisions? How are the costs and benefits of such decisions allocated? Questions are myriad, answers less numerous. Two generations into the era of African development, both positive and negative consequences of development efforts are apparent.

TABLE 5.8

Human Development

	1 GNP per Capita	2 GNP Rank	3 HDI	4 HDI Rank	5 GNP Rank minus HDI Rank
Angola	270	19	0.344	20	−1
Benin	350	14	0.378	13	1
Burkina Faso	230	22	0.219	29	−7
Burundi	170	27	0.241	27	0
Cameroon	610	8	0.481	6	2
CAR	310	16	0.347	19	−3
Chad	160	29	0.318	24	5
Congo	670	5	0.383	11	−6
Cote d'Ivoire	660	6	0.368	15	−9
Ethiopia	100	31	0.252	26	5
Gabon	3,950	1	0.568	4	−3
Ghana	360	12	0.473	7	5
Kenya	320	15	0.463	9	6
Lesotho	660	6	0.469	8	−2
Madagascar	250	20	0.348	18	2
Malawi	180	26	0.334	23	3
Mali	240	21	0.236	28	−7
Mauritania	470	11	0.361	16	−5
Mozambique	80	32	0.281	25	7
Namibia	2,250	3	0.644	2	1
Niger	200	24	0.207	30	−6
Nigeria	240	21	0.391	10	11
Senegal	570	10	0.342	21	−11
Sierra Leone	200	23	0.185	31	−8
South Africa	3,250	2	0.717	1	1
Swaziland	1,210	4	0.597	3	1
Tanzania	170	27	0.358	17	10
Togo	300	17	0.380	12	5
Uganda	300	17	0.340	22	−5
Zambia	360	12	0.378	13	−1
Zimbabwe	610	8	0.507	5	3

Table 5.8 compares actual wealth of African states to the quality of life as reported by the UNDP in its recent *Human Development Report*. There is far from a direct correlation between available income and "well-offness" (compare columns 2 and 4). Some explanations for this seeming paradox include the following: There is a very skewed distribution of wealth—i.e., a few very wealthy people control resources while the masses are poor. This could produce a fairly high per capita GDP without widespread wealth. Another explanation is that the government has resources but squanders them on weapons, conspicuous consumption, or offshore investments. A third explanation is that the elements of development measured by the UNDP are not those elements that the residents of a particular state want to see enhanced. Therefore, when provided with an opportunity, they use their resources for consumption that HDI does not reflect by, for example, purchasing television sets instead of investing in education or health care. The larger the negative number in column 5, the more the resources of that state are not being devoted to improving the factors that improve the HDI in the eyes of the UNDP.

It is not only those who have developed who should judge the value of those changes. Those who have not yet reached that objective must consider the value of the benefit, recognizing that a substantial down payment has already been made. The question is: Do they want to go "forward"?

NOTES

1. The United Nations uses three categories: low, middle, and high development.

2. "Images of Rural East Africa," *Fieldstaff Reports* 15, September, 1971: 8.

3. "Service" in this context is not cooking and cleaning, but fulfilling commercial needs other than with physical products—i.e., banking, insurance, stock trading.

4. Street vendors in our neighbourhood in Malawi offered almost exclusively Chinese merchandise, virtually all of it patently inferior to similar Western products. These goods are priced at a fraction of the cost of better quality mer-

chandise produced in a Western country, so people with very little disposable income opt for inferior products and become disillusioned by this waste of their money.

5. Discussing kitchen technology with a cook, I asked if he had seen a microwave oven, a technological advance that entered the U.S. market in the late 1970s. He did not know of it, and he explained that there was a 20–30-year time lag between a product's arrival in the American market and its appearance in Africa.

6. Former President F. W. DeKlerk acknowledged as much in remarks to the Indianapolis Economic Club, 17 September 1998.

7. To be precise, only four states extended diplomatic recognition to Biafra: France, Tanzania, Cote d'Ivoire, and Cameroon.

8. Discussing the devastating AIDS crisis with a West African physician, I asked why there was no sense of urgency in those states with HIV positivity rates in the range of 25%. He reflected for a moment and then replied: "In Africa we don't have the sense of urgency you have in the West." There is abundant evidence to sustain this assessment, and that goes a long way towards explaining the cultural gap between Africa and the West.

9. Construction of the railway produced several instances of neoimperialism. For example, once the Chinese promised the railroad, the United States, not to be outdone, promised a highway and the Italians a pipeline—all traversing the same corridor. A day came when Chinese and American contractors almost came to blows over the preferable route—in the Cold-War days when there was no contact between the two systems otherwise.

10. There was a gang burglary in the homes across the street from our house in Malawi, obviating all the protective systems. Discussing our options with our night watchman, Lashidi, we cautioned that we did not want him to risk harm in the face of overwhelming odds. His comment: "If my time has come, it has come. If I am killed while bicycling home this morning, and you say, 'I just talked to Lashidi!' you know that my time has come." Ironically, this is the same person who festooned our premises with seed pods, owl feathers, and small segments of vines in an effort to ward off evil. Consistency is no more prevalent in Africa than elsewhere!

11. Our hired auto had broken down in the highway outside Yaounde, Cameroon. Casting about for a solution to our problem, I suggested to our driver that he ask the driver of the log truck stopped behind us if he would tow us the 60 kilometers into town. "For $1,000" was the offer. Our driver's comment: "You can't trust those Francophone people!" "Ethnicity" takes all forms.

12. A European academic reported a conversation with the Governor of the Reserve Bank of Zambia: "You have been Governor for several years, but I have not heard your name linked to any scandals." The Governor's reply: "Now that the system has been deregulated there are no more opportunities for bribes!"

13. Classic examples of religious rejection of technological change are the

Amish communities in the northeastern and midwestern United States. Technology developed after a prescribed period is taboo.

14. Transparency International in Berlin reports annually on perceived corruption levels reported by business travelers. Nigeria is one of the most opaque at present.

15. I was struck in listening to the Malawian Broadcasting Company how predictable were the daily announcements that a government minister encouraged the citizens of some location to look to self-help projects to improve their lives, and not to look to government. This at least has the virtue of not raising unrealistic expectations.

16. Mazrui would extend the impact of slavery to include "humiliation," manifested in various forms of racism (p. 28).

CHAPTER 6

African Political Systems

How does a society survive and satisfy the needs of its citizens? Political systems are developed for the purpose of wielding state power to organize resources for the satisfaction of certain needs. These needs are communicated to the center from the periphery (or perhaps vice versa), and the receiver responds. On several levels, political systems exercise the power of life and death over the subjects

President Mobutu Sese Seko of Zaire. [1965–1997]

of the system. Nowhere is this more true than in Africa. When a substantial portion of the citizenry lives at the edge of subsistence, minor decisions made by the system can have major implications for a person's or a group's survival. For example, will government build a well or buy a computer? Will the well be here? Or there? Or will it be a road? The proper role of government is to employ its inherently limited resources in problem solving for its population. But the problems are usually identified by those who already have resources and seek to preserve and expand—rather than share—them. The political challenge is to prioritize problems to be addressed, and decide who should deal with them and for whose benefit.[1]

The government, or polity, is also the intermediary between the citizen, others within the same polity, and the rest of the world—neighboring states, distant states (including super-powers), regional entities, transnational corporations, other business interests, international organizations, etc. The polity is also its own intermediary between the people and its system in that it has to establish its own legitimacy in the eyes of its citizens. If it is to focus the power of the system effectively to meet needs and solve problems, it must be accepted as having the *right* to act. Usually this is termed legitimacy: The government is in power because it *deserves* to be there on the basis of some accepted measurement (see Box 4.1). It achieved power through an agreed-upon prior process; it adheres to agreed-upon rules in its use of power; and it responsibly represents (or is perceived to responsibly represent) all segments of the population. Obviously, there are many caveats to these requirements, but to the extent that these standards are *not* met, the system is said to lack legitimacy. Inherently, any system works toward homogenization of its society, as in controlling the educational process. Common solutions are often offered for differential problems and needs, which obviously works better for some groups than for others. The sensitivity of the regime to these differences affects its legitimacy in the eyes of the affected groups.

The establishment of modern political systems in the **West-ern model** depends upon recognition by the political elite of a state that the opposition can be as honest and reputable in seeking its objectives as the group or groups in power. Much of Africa's recent political history has consisted of the "us-versus-them" conflicts in which the opposition is demonized (whether that opposition is a colonial regime, insurgents, separatists, superpowers, or neighbors). It is often difficult to recognize that the legitimate political party in opposition to the group in power is just as entitled to be heard—or to take control of the government—as the party on the majority side of the system. Because tradition has emphasized consensual decision making in many African societies, the idea of arguing diametrically opposed positions taking the opposing opinion seriously, and giving each a similar chance to prevail does not go down well. Today efforts to develop "civic culture" are prevalent in many African states as they flirt with demo-

WESTERN MODEL

This describes a political/economic system similar to those found in the industrial West. These systems are generally referred to politically as liberal democracies and as capitalist or democratic socialist in terms of economics. Politically, there are "free and fair" elections with orderly changes of government when the opposition wins. There is free speech, a free press, freedom of assembly, and unrestrained practice of religion. Individuals and their rights are respected. Both presidential and parliamentary systems conform to this model.

The Western economic model is a combination of capitalism and socialism. A free market operates, but a social safety net exists which includes education, health care, and provision for the very young, very old, and disabled. Free trade and protection of business interests are also typical.

BOX 6.1

cratic processes and principles, but democracy develops only over time. If it is a practice contrary to longstanding tradition, it takes root very slowly. "Civic culture" consists of the invisible set of relationships that allow people to engage in political discourse and to arrive at decisions about their common concerns and ideals. Even when the civic culture is strong, the transition to the political uncertainty of a democratic system is precarious in the face of domestic or international instability.

The Carter Center tabulates the number of "democratic" regimes in Africa at any given time. In 1995 their count was fifteen with another six "directed democracies." Sixteen were in transition to democracy, and six exhibited an "ambiguous commitment" to democracy. Three states were termed "authoritarian," and nine were experiencing "contested sovereignty.[6] None of these "conditions" can be assumed to be permanent. The transitory nature of African regimes is seen by the 1991 finding of the Carter Center: eight democracies were identified along with three directed democracies, five states with a "strong" commitment to democracy, thirteen with a moderate commitment; fifteen governments were ambiguous; seven authoritarian, and four were undergoing contested sovereignty.

The data in table 6.1 indicate in general terms the measure of democracy in African governments. Elections alone are not valid indicators of political participation. Women's eligibility to participate or even their participation in parliament does not indicate social or economic equality.

The South African program "Democracy For All" enumerates thirteen "signposts of democracy:" (1) citizen participation; (2) equality regardless of race, religion, etc.; (3) political tolerance; (4) accountability of officials; (5) transparency in government operation; (6) regular, free, and fair elections; (7) economic freedom including choosing one's own work and labor union membership; (8) control of the abuse of power including avoidance of corruption; (9) a bill of rights guaranteed to citizens; (10) acceptance of election results; (11) guaranteed human rights; (12) effective multipartyism; and (13) the rule of law.[2] This program is

TABLE 6.1

Democracy in Africa

State	1 Number of Political Parties in Legislature (most recent election)	2 Year Women Received Right to Vote	3 Year First Woman Elected to Parliament	4 Democracy Status According to Carter Criteria
Angola	11 (1992)	1975*	1980	contested sovereignty
Benin	6 (1995)	1956	1979	democratic
Botswana	2 (1994)	1965	1979	democratic
Burkina Faso	4 (1997)	1958	1978	directed democracy
Burundi	—	1961	1982	contested sovereignty
Cameroon	4 (1997)	1946	1960	directed democracy
CAR	12 (1993)	1986	1987	democratic
Chad	10 (1997)	1958	1962	ambiguous commitment
Congo	None	1963	1963	democratic
Cote d'Ivoire	2 (1995)	1952	1965	ambiguous commitment
Djibouti	1 (1997)	1946	None	ambiguous commitment
Eritrea	—	1955	1994	moderately committed
Ethiopia	2 (1995)	1955	1957	moderately committed
Gabon	6 (1996)	1956	1961	moderately committed
Gambia	4 (1997)	1960	1982	ambiguous commitment
Ghana	4 (1996)	1954	—	moderately committed
Guinea	5 (1995)	1958	1963	directed democracy
Guinea-Bissau	5 (1994)	1977	None	moderately committed

Country				
Kenya	10 (1997)	1963	1969	[ambiguous commitment]
Lesotho	1 (1993)	1965	None	moderately committed
Madagascar	16 (1993)	1959	1965	democratic
Malawi	3 (1999)	1961	1964	[directed democracy]
Mali	8 (1997)	1956	1964	democratic
Mauritania	—	—	—	moderately committed
Mozambique	3 (1994)	1975	1977	moderately committed
Namibia	5 (1994)	1989	1989	democratic
Niger	4 (1996)	1948	1989	democratic
Nigeria	— (1999)	1958	—	democratic
Senegal	6 (1993)	1945	1963	democratic
Sierra Leone	—	1961	—	contested sovereignty
South Africa	7 (1999)	1930*	1933	democratic
Sudan	—	1964	1964	contested sovereignty
Swaziland	—	1968	1972	ambiguous commitment
Tanzania	5 (1995)	1959	—	moderately committed
Togo	5 (1994)	1945	1961	directed democracy
Uganda	1 (1996)	1962	1962	moderately committed
Zaire	—	1967	1970	contested sovereignty
Zambia	4 (1996)	1962	1964	democratic
Zimbabwe	2 (1995)	1957	1980	ambiguous commitment

Sources: United Nations. *Human Development Report 1998*; Carter Center, *Africa Demos*, III: 4 March, 1995. Brackets [ ] indicate adjustments by the author to account for changes since these data were originally published. Publication of *Africa Demos* has been discontinued.

*Only the white population voted.

PATRICE LUMUMBA

Patrice Lumumba, a postal clerk in the Belgian Congo, took the lead in establishing a postcolonial regime. An announced socialist, he was vigorously opposed by the United States and others in the West. Ultimately, he was murdered in a rebellion supported by the Central Intelligence Agency.

BIOBOX 6.1

supported by the United States Agency for International Development, so it is not surprising that it mirrors what one would find in a similar listing in this country.

Only in Liberia and Ethiopia where there were no colonial regimes are the political systems generally free of European influence. Gordon (p. 61) reminds us that the colonial powers departed abruptly in part to prevent the emergence of a radicalized anticolonial leadership (the very existence of which had been provoked and energized by colonial abuses). However, in the case of the most abrupt departure—that of Belgium from the Congo—the first elections produced just such a radical leader, Patrice Lumumba. Cold War concerns prompted the United States to support his removal from power, and he was eventually replaced by President Mobutu with the collaboration of the CIA. While left-leaning leadership was tolerated in some states—e.g., Nyerere in Tanzania—the Congo (later Zaire, and then Congo again) was seen as strategic because of its size, location, and mineral wealth; and thus was a crucial pawn in the Cold War.

POLITICS AND POVERTY

Human nature being what it is, it did not take long for elements of authoritarianism to emerge, many in uniparty states. The single party was usually intolerant of disagreement, and was often willing to manipulate the strings of power to the disadvantage of opponents—not to mention its own advantage—often with implicit or explicit outside support. Given the powers of the public purse and of government appointments as well as international connections, it was often irresistible for uniparty regimes to bolster their own prestige and bank accounts as well as those of their friends at the public's expense. This situation characterizes much of Africa's postindependence politics.

Simple arithmetic demonstrates how it is possible for the poor to remain poor while the rich move ahead. That gap widens at the state level. Table 6.2 hypothesizes two states, "R" rich and "P" poor. Actually, it is based upon the average data for two groups from the United Nations *Human Development Report 1994*. Even though the hypothesized difference in growth rate is a minuscule two-tenths of 1 percent, the compounding effect over a ten-year period—on top of the vast initial differences—is remarkable. Given the enormous gap between the typical rich and poor states, normal rates of growth are not sufficient to enable the poor to catch up within an average lifetime, and certainly not within the "political lifetime" of any given leader. Extraordinary measures must be sought, as we have seen in China over the past decade. Asian comparisons with Africa, however, are highly questionable for historical, cultural, political, and strategic reasons. In actuality, growth rates for Africa overall averaged 1.4 percent in 1991–94, not the 2.8 percent hypothesized; for the rich states, growth rates averaged about 5 percent—not 3 percent. There have been improvements in recent years in some states, but not enough to bridge this gap.

What national-level statistics fail to illustrate, however, is the sizable disparities contained *within* those general figures. For example, figure 6.1 shows the very great differences between two Nigerian states, Bendel and Borno. The gap between the rich and poor in Nigeria is comparable to the global disparity between South and North—e.g., more than US$16,000 GDP per capita for the 64 "high development" states compared to US$1,362 for

TABLE 6.2
Hypothesised GNP Growth Rates for Rich and Poor States

	Annual GNP Growth Rate	Year 2	Year 3	Year 4	Year 5	Year 6	Year 7	Year 8	Year 9
"R" 3%	$14,860	15,306	15,765	16,238	16,725	17,227	17,744	18,276	18,824
"P" 2.8%	$880	905	930	956	983	1010	1039	1068	1098
Gap	$13,980	14,401	14,835	15,282	15,742	16217	16,705	17,208	17,726
Increase in Gap	—	421	434	447	460	475	488	503	518
(Percent)	—	(3.011%)	(3.014%)	(3.013%)	(3.010%)	(3.017%)	(3.009%)	(3.011%)	(3.010%)

Source: World Bank, *World Development Report 1989*, p. 151.

"low development" states. It is a reflection of the two major impediments to African modernization—maladaptive culture and neoimperialism. The wealthy have often—though not in every instance—mastered the art of exploiting the global economy to their own advantage: i.e., they have adapted to playing by the rules of a prevailing culture other than their indigenous culture. In moving into the global culture (read, "economy"), the economic elite generally participate in neoimperialist practices, because the massive reservoirs of wealth at the disposal of this elite are provided by entities outside Africa and augmented by the surplus labor pool available at home.

FIGURE 6.1

Disparities within Nigeria: Two States

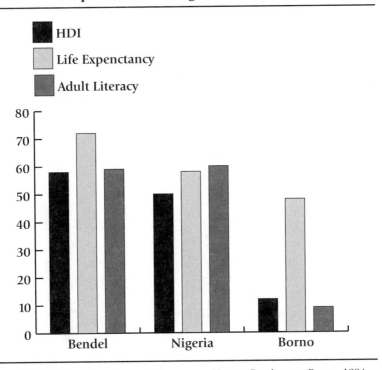

Source: United Nations Development Programme, *Human Development Report*, 1994.

Over time a variety of regimes adopted the uniparty typology, but they separated into six distinct types (see Chazan, others). None encouraged political opposition, but their degree of responsiveness to popular concerns varied. Differences lay in the mechanisms they employed to extract loyalty and resources from their respective populations; all exhibited basic uniparty characteristics:

- **Administrative-Hegemonial ("praetorian")**—This system is built on a military foundation with generals and politicians collaborating in managing affairs of state. The symbiotic relationship between the two is mutually reinforcing. The military sector benefits from business dealings with the private sector, and businesses are protected by the military. Examples include Sergeant Rawlings' Ghana, several Nigerian regimes, and even to some extent South Africa prior to majority rule. These governments operate not in response to perceived popular needs, but as mechanisms which employ the power of the state to sustain the elite.
- **Party-mobilizing**—The classic example of this system was Tanzania under Nyerere. His party, TANU (Tanzanian African National Union), was effectively the government. No political competition was permitted (though there was intraparty contention for nominations). Delivery of government services was filtered through the party, and the lines between the government and the party were, at best, blurred. So long as the benign Nyerere "ruled," all was well; but a less principled leader could easily have become autocratic and created a party-centralist system. In a very different way, Botswana operates with a strong uniparty system, but because of its diamond income, it can still respond to popular needs, and it relies less on compulsion than do many states.
- **Party-centralist**—This system is manifested in KANU (Kenyan African National Union). KANU was the winner

of a political contest with KADU (D=Democratic), each party led by a charismatic personality who emerged from anticolonial agitation. In this case, the intention of Jomo Kenyatta, who triumphed, was not to deliver services effectively nor mobilize the populace, but to centralize control, wealth, and power in the hands of the party. He succeeded, and his role was passed on at his death to Vice-President Arap Moi.

- **Personal-coercive**—The most senior regime and leader in Africa (until his removal in 1997) was the leader of the MPR (*Mouvement Populaire Revolutionaire*), President (and *Foundateur de la Republique*) Mobutu Sese Sekou. Installed in collaboration with the Central Intelligence Agency in 1965, President Mobutu managed his **kleptocracy** adroitly.[3]

KLEPTOCRACY

The Greek roots of this word are "thief" and "rule"—i.e., rule by thievery. It was coined, I believe, by an observer of a Latin American dictator who pilfered on a grand scale. In Africa the description was regularly applied to the government of President Mobutu of Zaire. He claimed—and outside observers supported his assertion—a fortune of US$5 billion which he acquired over his thirty years as Zaire's leader. This sum was not amassed by mere pilfering. Mobutu treated the national treasury as his personal account, drawing cash whenever he decided to buy another villa in Europe or order up a plane belonging to the national airline to take him wherever he decided to go—for example, to France for a haircut! The airline's consequent unreliability was such that a private alternative airline arose to maintain a semblance of scheduled service for those relatively few government, IGO, NGO, and business people who flew in and out of Zaire.

BOX 6.2

In order to satisfy his massive appetite for material possessions and adulation, he united the party and the government in an efficient mechanism through which he coerced
the populace to comply with his demands. Another example is Hastings Banda's thirty-year rule in Malawi. People
were discouraged from constructing new houses (actually
mud huts with thatched roofs) because that would set
them in competition with the leader. Dissidents regularly
disappeared or died in mysterious auto accidents. Banda
prohibited the teaching of political science in the university for fear of disturbing the balance. His wealth included large tracts of farmland and several palaces.

- **Populist**—In Liberia, the early days of Sergeant Samuel
  Doe's regime was populist. Reacting to and rebelling
  against a small oligarchy of "Liberio-Americans" descended
  from repatriated slaves, the "people" rose up and over-
  turned the elite government in favor of a sergeant-leader. As
  is too regularly the case, populism turned into authoritarianism, power corrupted, and Liberia was transformed once
  again into an autocracy before it collapsed into anarchy.

- **Pluralist**—The wave of democracy that is purportedly
  sweeping Africa is predicated upon pluralist principles, the
  open and tolerant competition of competing ideas and
  institutions. This is ostensibly the case in Botswana where
  fairly open opposition can be seen in parliament and in the
  press. Since the route to power in Botswana is through
  diamond mining and marketing, however, real economic
  power is not so widely spread, and there is an economic
  oligarchy. Still, there is greater equality, both political and
  economic, in that state than anywhere else in Africa. Also,
  perhaps South Africa can sustain the pluralist system
  established there in 1994.

- **Chaotic**—This condition is illustrated by periods in the
  history of Somalia, Sierra Leone, Liberia, and Rwanda (and
  Zaire has returned to this condition, as it did in the

1960s). In this circumstance, public order breaks down and there is no recognized legitimate authority. Management by force leads to the rule of the gun, to precolonial or colonial arrangements, or to some combination thereof. Infrastructure generally deteriorates or is destroyed, and development is measurably curtailed.

Acceptance of legitimate opposition, the recognition that another opinion can reasonably coexist with the dominant one, and the idea that election losers quietly retire from the fray are not part of the African tradition. Until these ideas take root, it is unlikely that democratic systems will flourish.

POLITICS AND PROBLEMS

The problems faced by most African governments have little to do with any particular political system despite propaganda to the contrary. Much more pressing in terms of daily decisions are the people's demands for food, jobs, and social services (education, health care). In the tradition inherited from the colonial era, the government was seen as the enemy, not a facilitator for improving citizens' lives. Leaders who advanced under colonial rule were often unacceptable when independence was attained: they had collaborated with the enemy. As a matter of fact, many of the first leaders of independent states were involved to some extent in anticolonial opposition.[4]

The colonial boundaries which created multiethnic states also created other types of divisions—e.g., religious, linguistic, physical—which were relevant to political and cultural issues. In some cases—e.g., Sudan, Zaire, Nigeria[5]—there are or have been efforts at secession by substantial ethnic minorities, as Eritrea seceded from Ethiopia in 1991. At a minimum, the cultural differences among the several groups within a single state have implications for all activities of government, especially those involving equity and justice. On occasion, external interference complicates matters even further.

The Western ideal of the democratic state requires not only stability—and hence a level of economic well-being that allows citizens to attend to political concerns—but also a tradition that accepts transfers of power, criticism and disagreement, change and uncertainty. These are not political practices or traditions generally found in African traditions, and they cannot simply be imposed or adopted. They have to evolve over time in a process of cultural adaptation and evaluation. While that evolution is proceeding, however, there are immediate problems over which the states have little or no control: drought, population pressures (carrying capacity), health concerns, regional disorder, and foreign interference which requires an immediate response. The impact of these problems pushes the drive for democracy to the background.

It is unlikely that Western-style democracy will successfully emerge in Africa for many years to come. There are, and will continue to be, efforts to institute democratic *practices*, but democratic *culture* develops gradually, regardless of external pressure.[7] Van Donge observes that democratic elections conflict with a traditional notion, at least in some areas, that assumes consensus to be the natural state, making it difficult to accommodate defeat.[8]

Despite universal acclaim for the democratic election of Nelson Mandela in South Africa, the socioeconomic reality he had to confront could not simply be resolved by a democratic election. Furthermore, the election of Mandela was not an authentic example of democracy because he was a folkloric hero supported by most of the world for his resistance to a reactionary system in disrepute and disarray. Future South African elections will better test how well democracy is entrenched in the South African political system.

For now, with a substantial portion of the electorate unemployed, homeless, and alienated from the system, only a generous infusion of resources can possibly turn their fortunes around. And while South Africa is the continent's richest state, producing about half its gross national product, it cannot control a declining world gold market, and Mandela found himself unable to fulfill constituent expectations for jobs, land, housing, health care, education, and crucial AIDS prevention. As this is written South Africa has completed a second round of elections, but political disenchantment appears to be growing.

If ways to engender economic activity in Africa are not found, continued instability and worse may define the future. As pressures increase both internally and externally, regimes that are viewed as authoritarian can anticipate increasing difficulties in obtaining aid, investment, and international influence.

With the failure of many African systems since the conflict structure of the Cold War collapsed, the case for autonomous development of an African style of government becomes stronger. It is now less important to conform in name to democracy or capitalism simply to satisfy the West, and it becomes more important to seek authenticity in meeting the needs and expectations of the populations. As the international community continues to develop higher levels of human rights expectations, it will be increasingly possible to rely on external forces to restrain government misbehavior and to sustain responsible government. For example, the United Nations' creation of an International Criminal Court in response to the atrocities in Rwanda and Bosnia may serve as a brake on government excesses. The unrestrained exercise of U.S. power in several places can also send the message that "big brother is watching"—if only from a distance, and if only in big brother's own self-interest!

NOTES

1. Harold Lasswell defines politics as: "who gets what, when, and how" in a book of that title, published by P. Smith, New York, 1936.

2. Enumerated in "Democracy Watch" 4, 1998.

3. Recognition of corruption, in this case unofficial, came in an advertisement placed by the Central Bank of Nigeria in several publications in 1997: "You Have Been Warned." It documented a long-running fraud originating in Nige-

ria in which individuals in the West were contacted regarding potential business schemes requiring "up-front" payments for taxes, legal fees, etc. See, for example, *The Economist*, 13 September 1997, p. 21. London police report at least 18,000 complaints of this type, including one from the Director of the Serious Fraud Office who was offered $9.6 million for his participation! (*Africa Analysis* 240, 20 September 1996).

4. Kenneth Kaunda of Zambia, Kwame Nkrumah of Ghana, Sekou Touré of Guinea, Jomo Kenyatta of Kenya, Ahmadou Ahidjo of Cameroon, and Eduardo Mondlane of Mozambique, among others.

5. As this is written, Sudan is still beset by a 20-year rebellion by Christian Bantu southerners against Moslem Arab northerners. Katanga Province in southeastern Zaire attempted to rebel in the 1960s, and the current instability in former Zaire may portend another attempt. In 1967, the Ibo-dominated southeast portion of Nigeria, Biafra, declared independence, but there was little international support and the effort collapsed. Recent years have seen a renewal of hostilities by the military government.

6. See, inter alia, table 6.1 and Carol Lancaster, "Democracy in Africa," *Foreign Policy* (Winter) 1991.

7. James Zaffiro, in remarks at the African Studies Association meeting, Chicago, October, 1998, observes that effective mass media are a necessary, but not sufficient, condition for the survival of democracy.

8. Jan VanDonge, seminar, University of Malawi, September, 1997.

CHAPTER 7

African Images of Self: Modernization in the Twentieth Century

> For who else would teach rhythm to the world
> that has died of machines and cannons?
>
> —Leopold Sedar Senghor

One author introduced Africa with this: "I greet you in silence." Elementary psychology asserts that how social beings see themselves goes a long way toward determining how they are perceived by others, how they behave, and even how their social institutions develop. Africa, the dark continent in many lexicons, certainly demonstrated this in the era of colonialism and continues to do so today—in another era of colonialism.

Until the nineteenth century, Africa was largely unknown outside itself. There were few reasons for outsiders to penetrate Africa, and fewer still for Africans to leave the continent on a large scale. The exceptions to this rule were Arab traders who visited the Indian Ocean coast for hundreds of years prior to a European presence there. These traders' legacy was largely replaced by the more recent influx of workers imported from British India to serve the colonial empire as laborers. Many of these workers remained to become the merchant class in much of East and South Africa.

WHICH IMAGE IS AFRICA?

These Dinka shepherds from Sudan follow an age-old pattern as they bring their cattle to the river to graze and drink.

President Blaise Compaoré of Burkina Faso holds a modern political press conference.

To this day, there remains in the minds of some—Africans and non-Africans alike—a Kiplingesque **image** of European relations vis-à-vis Africa, frequently more subtle and nuanced than overt and explicit:

IMAGE

Much of life, especially in the political arena, is a matter not only of objective reality but of an *image* of reality. We act upon what we *see*, but we may not see what actually *is*. Much of the civil life of Africa operates on the basis of limited vision. Large portions of any population are politically illiterate because of limited education and lack of relevant experience. Most locales suffer from a dearth of accessible information; availability of newspapers and magazines is limited, and often only government-controlled electronic media are received. So the available images are subject to limitations, distortion, and outright manipulation.

The message sent is equally unreliable. Political leaders frequently attempt to appear more powerful than they are—e.g., by surrounding themselves with trappings of power (fancy automobiles, grand houses, elegant dress, hosts of servants, etc.). To the impoverished masses, the social distance created magnifies that leader's power, even in a kleptocratic (see box 6.3) state such as Zaire under Mobutu.

Then there is the matter of intent: If one seeks to delude, or if one seeks not to believe, images are further distorted. When all these variables are combined, the potential for perceptual mischief is substantial. **Example:** Emperor Jean Bedel Bokassa of the Central African Empire was eminently concerned with image, as was demonstrated in his coronation worthy of Louis XIV. Among the powerful, Mercedes Benz autos are very popular because they contribute to the owner's "image."

BOX 7.1

CHAPTER 7

Take up the White man's burden—
Send forth the best ye breed—
Go bind your sons to exile
To serve the captives' need;
To wait in heavy harness
On fluttered folk and wild—
Your new-caught sullen peoples,
Half devil and half child.

This was—and is—more than literary expostulation. To this day many argue that Africa is incapable of development.

To become "European" in today's world is to become "universal." Examine a photograph of a contemporary African city, the largest of which may house 30 percent of an African state's total population.[1] If the photo was taken with the intent of "sanitizing" the view—e.g., if it is a picture postcard—careful scrutiny may be required to differentiate it from a European or North American city of similar climate. Now thirty or more years into independence, African cities and the societies that populate them are becoming more and more European. Both the styles and the technology of Europe (i.e., of the West) are eagerly sought by Africans, regardless of their cultural or social implications. At the same time these cities are degrading both physically and socially because of overpopulation and lack of infrastructure maintenance.

The very *idea* of the modern city incorporates Western civilization and depreciates many elements of African tradition— e.g., closeness to the land and to extended families; strong sense of community. Reinforced by philosophical, economic, and religious traditions, Western cultural institutions have recast Africa. The tripartite individualism resulting from the renaissance, capitalism, and Christianity (to paraphrase Martin Luther, ". . . every man his own priest . . .") produced a complete reorientation of African epistemology among those who subscribed. This was rewarded by success in the institutions of the West—promotion in business, success in academic pursuits, ordination into the clergy, all avenues to power and prestige.

WILLIE ABRAHAM

Willie Abraham was a Ghanian philosopher. Trained in England, he sought to interpret Africa's contemporary situation in terms that would have meaning for intellectuals around the world.

BIOBOX 7.1

The city in Africa attracted those who were ambitious, skilled, or otherwise convinced that they could make it in the more dynamic and competitive environment of the Western-dominated system. Left behind were the old, the very young, often the women, and the uncompetitive. Urban life evolved its own national or cosmopolitan culture which supplanted traditional practices and values. The consequent weakening of tribal and religious values strengthened national identity.

As Africans saw the largesse attendant on success, the desire to achieve it was reinforced time and again. While many in Africa may rail against the perversions of Western materialism or Western excesses, we are still flattered by imitation, if not by accolade. Even those who have attempted to articulate an alternative style—most elaborately, President Mobutu of Zaire with his *authenticité*[2]—have failed to successfully confront the trend. No cultural system has equaled that of the West in its mass appeal to Africans.

Other voices are raised against unquestioning acceptance of everything European. African writer Willie Abraham observed that the "white man's myth of superiority was cracking through seeing his failings." Not all examples of Western culture were salutary, and egregious examples were often seized upon to denigrate all things associated with the West. The most regularly cited example is probably the slave trade, which Abraham suggests is

Africa's price for sharing Europe's intellectual revolution (p. 131). (Think back to the cost/benefit analysis of colonies.) While many African leaders can be faulted for excesses (Mobutu, Amin, Bokassa, Banda, Doe, Abacha, Mengistu), a cursory glance at history brings non-Africans to mind as well: Hitler, Verwoerd, Marcos, Batista, and Pol Pot—Africans none of them, but similarly malign. So the categorizing of Africa in deprecating terms has been reversed by some to make categorical judgments more complex as well as more balanced from their perspective.

One persistent problem of both colonial and postindependence regimes was the acquisition of legitimacy. The state did not often rest upon a base of strong popular support or historical reality; often both the colonial entity and the subsequent states were conceived in violence, with the government resting more upon compulsion than upon consent. Unable to exercise the same level of technological and social control as Hitler's Germany or Communist China, African excesses became better known. Coupled with the predilection of some toward racial prejudice, this caused African leadership to be ridiculed, and the problem was compounded by the relative poverty of African states. Legitimacy was indeed elusive.

THE INTERNATIONAL ARENA

The great leap into the international arena at the time of independence ran counter to these traditional African values, which are generally introspective:

1. Beyond the extended *family*, there are extended *relationships* not acknowledged in Western societies.
2. Much land is communally held, creating an economic and legal system totally unlike that of the individualistic West.
3. Close physical relationships, as between mother and child, are valued and fostered. Think of the babies carried practically full-time on their mothers' backs.

4. Economic organization is group-oriented, not exclusivist: e.g., hunting, gathering, herding.
5. Belief systems emphasize tradition such as the "chain of life" which enables Zaïrians to name sixteen generations of ancestors.[3]
6. Inherently, the poor and the pastoral are more closely engaged with their environments than they could be in a society in which human-natural relationships are intermediated by vast and complex technology (e.g., air conditioning, vehicles, medicines).
7. African cultures are like other cultures in that they seek to control change. This means that they do not accept change wholesale. The pace and content of cultural change is controlled by elaborately evolved traditions.
8. Abraham points out that the Akan, for example, view the power to rule as derived from the people and held in trust for them (p. 75), not as a confirmation of one's personal accomplishment or worth.
9. Mazrui describes African **nationalism** as more egalitarian than libertarian. This constitutes the basis for political systems and philosophy more completely than many acknowledge.

Western values were not needed to replace or supplant African values on a wholesale basis as if there had been a cultural vacuum in Africa. Indeed, some cultural features paralleled widely-held Western values, but they were interpreted differently because of the very different historical and material endowments of African societies. Different is neither better nor worse; it is simply "different." How well social institutions serve a society as it pursues its values must be judged in light of the values being pursued.

In colonial Africa, there was a general expectation by both Europeans and Africans of one-way cultural adaptation—from black to white ("glazed with the white clay of foreign education," from one observer's perspective). Only in the most recent times has there been anything akin to mutuality in African-Western rela-

NATIONALISM

While having my shoes shined by a lad in Ethiopia many years ago, I took out my Amharic phrase book and said, as best I could, "I am an American." I was attempting to make some minimal conversation and to differentiate myself from Canadians he might encounter. The shoe shiner stood tall and announced, "I am an Ethiopian." In doing so, he demonstrated a ubiquitous sentiment—pride in country, or nationalism.

It is a universal truism that most people have a particularly strong feeling for their own country. (This is a particularly useful emotion if they are expected to pay taxes or are called into battle and asked to die for their country.) This sentiment can be fostered by governments to develop allegiance (sometimes "blind" allegiance) to one's country. It is one thing to strongly identify oneself as a citizen of Slabovia and to be proud of the nation's history and culture; it is a very short leap to believe that Slabovians are superior to all other forms of life. When that happens (as in Hitler's Germany, to take an extreme example), the consequences can be deadly. But in order to create a nation out of disparate bits and pieces left from colonial regimes, African states have had to work very hard at developing a sense of nationalism.

Once nationalism takes hold, it can become reified. That is, from identifying with a country, one moves on to identify that country with a particular leader. This has happened in several African nations—e.g., President Kenyatta of Kenya. Nationalism then becomes a necessary evil. Without it, the populace lacks the enthusiasm to support the system; with too much of it, the people can become hostile to other neighbors or to domestic political opponents.

BOX 7.2

tionships. The search for traditional cures by Western-trained physicians, for example, suggests a new reciprocity that was wholly absent in earlier times. It was ignorantly assumed that everything European was superior and preferable to everything African, with no prior critical examination. This resulted in the imposition of everything European and the depreciation of everything African. Aside from whatever inefficiencies and losses this produced, it took a great social toll on Africans, who saw everything they had been taught to value over the ages dismissed, discarded, and repressed by those in power.

Abraham takes a moderate view of the incipient ennui likely to be produced by such attitudes: "Through judicious grafting one may avoid some of the excesses which have been associated with a lopsided expansion of material culture in Europe." When reduced to its philosophical context, Western society can appear (and does appear to many) to be nothing more than a society of materialists lacking redeeming spiritual virtues, though there are those who would argue the point differently.[4]

This leads us to the specific condemnation by Chinua Achebe who asserts that the Christian converts of his acquaintance in Nigerian society were the failures of their communities. His fictionalized version of the nexus of Christianity and African tradition illustrates this argument, and certainly it is true in some instances. Whether or not it is more generally true remains to be answered by others. Can change be accomplished selectively? Malinowski argues that "[Africans] only want [to integrate into modern life] what seems valuable from the past" (p. 157). Seen more pragmatically by Mamadou Dia,

> Colonial governments came to be damned not so much because they had ruthlessly upset the old order—although they were damned for that too—as because they had so inadequately carried through the work of industrializing ancient societies and dragooning them into the modern world. (p. 3)

In the end, the question remains: Which is it? Can a society be changed or change selectively? Must a society be *either* African or European? Has history evolved sufficiently for us to make that determination?

The oral tradition which replaced written history in most of Africa (at least in part because of the shortage of wood for producing paper and the inhospitable climate for paper) was misunderstood. Myths were perpetuated as language could be twisted to serve the purposes of both the hearers and repeaters of a story. When Europe and Africa met intellectually, it is not surprising that

INSIGHT: A NOTE ON CULTURAL RELATIVISM*

Cultural relativism, long a key concept in anthropology, asserts that every culture has its own values and practices, and that anthropologists should not make value judgments about cultural differences. As a result, anthropology stresses the value-free study of customs and norms. Today, however, this view is challenged, especially by those who want to take a stand on human rights issues.

In 1947 leaders of the American Anthropological Association withdrew from discussions on the Universal Declaration of Human Rights in the belief that no such declaration would be appropriate to all human beings. Anthropologists readily denounced Nazi genocide and South African *apartheid*, but other practices have not drawn such a clear response. The practice of female genital mutilation (clitoridectomy, also called female circumcision) has not been condemned, nor has the communal violence between Hindu and Muslim in India or Hutu and Tutsi in Rwanda.

In the Sudan, female circumcision often causes chronic infections and renders intercourse or childbirth horribly painful and difficult. However, Sudanese culture holds that an the Europeans dismissed African oral history as less believable than what had been reified in writing in European traditions. That, however, preceded the days of revisionist history, and it is now widely acknowledged that the Western written record is not inherently fairer or more accurate than the oral one.

The postcolonial political systems created by European imposition were not inherently stable, despite all the trappings of legitimacy with which they were cloaked. The impression of European political liberalism overlay an indigenous system with a very different style, though with many of the same essential objec-

---

uncircumcised woman is not respectable. Under British rule, the practice was outlawed in 1946, but that served only to take it underground and make it more dangerous.

The 1993 Human Rights Conference in Vienna declared circumcision to be a violation of the rights of children and of the women who suffer its effects for a lifetime. The issue was thus cast as something larger than the practice of a single culture. Other similar practices such as a Japanese wife's suicide in response to a husband's infidelity are tolerated, but for the betrayed wife to take the lives of her children would be viewed as murder.

Crosscultural exchanges have broadened the definition of human rights to address domestic violence, rights of cultural minorities, and the individual right to be free from threat or harm.

Given a choice between defending human rights and defending cultural relativism, anthropologists (and other students of culture) should choose to protect and promote human rights. We cannot just be bystanders.

---

*Adapted with permission from an article by Carolyn Fluehr-Lobban, *The Chronicle of Higher Education*, 9 June 1995.

tives. Nyerere reminds us, for example, that liberal democracy is a slowly acquired habit, and a system cannot reasonably be expected to be transformed into a full-blown liberal democracy the day after the colonial flag is replaced with a new one. As a matter of fact, one of the most pervasive and enduring legacies of the colonial period has been the oligarchy which was, in effect, inherited from the colonial regimes. "The concept of an institutionalised opposition and elections are altogether incomprehensible with social (kinship and communal) values as well as with the hereditary principles and religious values about leadership," as a South African scholar contends.[5]

INDEPENDENCE

In most places independence emerged out of tension. It had been preceded by a very gradual process of Africanization in many areas of life—the council chambers, the boardroom, the classroom—depending upon the desires and tolerance of the metropole. Since meritocracy as well as stability, efficiency, and profit necessitated that these positions be filled by well-qualified individuals—and since some of them risked alienating their peers by being considered collaborationists—the rewards to the individuals who occupied these positions were relatively substantial. Upon independence, the ultimate control of a transnational business, for example, did not change, nor did its visible [African] leadership. But under cover of local direction it became possible for many "managers" to exploit their advantage to gain even greater advantages, thereby entrenching politico-economic oligarchies in most states.

The African "front" for a multinational investment becomes the logical collaborator for additional future investments. And the very small economic oligarchy can collaborate to manipulate both political and economic situations to their further advantage.

Eastern and Southern Africa were home to another economic, but not political, oligarchy—the Asians. As successful laborers, they accumulated wealth, and—in accordance with their cultural traditions—moved into the role of traders from Kenya through South Africa. Their domination of the retail market is such that in many eastern and southern African cities and towns it is virtually impossible to conduct retail business other than with Asians. Their wealth makes them significant players behind the scenes and causes them to be disliked because of the perceived exclusion of Africans as petit traders. In a typical postcolonial city, the major economic enterprises—banks, manufacturing, hotels, large-scale agriculture—are multinational, generally owned by interests in the metropole. Small merchants are Asian, and street vendors and market people are African. There are other non-indigenous merchants from Greece and Lebanon as well as a few remaining colonials scattered throughout Africa. And, there are, of course, exceptions.

Another political tradition also resulted from the independence process—rebelliousness. Political leaders had, for perhaps two generations, agitated for independence through various attacks—verbal, economic, or physical—on the de facto order. The political lesson taught the citizenry that when a political system is unacceptable, it is appropriate to attack. Innumerable coups and revolutions have plagued independent Africa. In most places, there is still no unassailably legitimate, representative, prosperous system comparable to Western Europe's or North America's. Nor is there an immediate prospect that such will emerge in the foreseeable future.

Mongo Beti put it this way:

> In our times, if a White man said to you, "Get down on your knees," you didn't have anything better to do. . . Today, with your sons, it is no longer the same thing. They have grown; they scorn us because we have bent our backs in front of the Whites. (from *Ville Cruelle*, 1954)

In the early days of African independence in the 1950s, when only a few states could realistically contemplate **sovereignty**, *Negritude* was a widely-discussed theme accompanying other political developments. Thinking that in unity there would be enhanced strength, several African leaders in the Western hemisphere, along with African expatriates in England, convened a series of conferences culminating in 1945 in Manchester. There, efforts were made to develop a unified front to confront colonialism. While this enjoyed a limited success in the arts, it was never particularly effective politically. Every conceivable kind of impediment existed to the concept of Negritude *cum* Pan-Africanism. The hard realities of international politics, especially in the era of the Cold War, did not leave much space for ideologies that were not immediately relevant to survival, and most of these specific African concerns moved silently into the background.[6] Even at the end of the Cold War, there is no place for Pan-Africanism. The

SOVEREIGNTY

Sovereignty is the political counterpart of autarchy in the realm of economics. A state subject to no higher authority is sovereign. A region within a state—e.g., Provence in France or Kwazulu-Natal in South Africa—is, by definition, not sovereign. On the other hand, Gambia or Mauritius is, by definition, sovereign regardless of the limitation on the exercise of that sovereignty in the international system. The very definition of a sovereign state is that it is the political equal of every other sovereign state and enjoys the same rights and responsibilities under international law, so the West was neither surprised nor averse to sustaining this crucial element of the Western political system as Africa became independent and African states claimed their sovereignty.

BOX 7.3

pressures of globalization, debt, multinational businesses, and regional politics have repressed the once powerful pull that Pan-Africanism and Negritude exerted.

While struggling to achieve economic development with the affluent West as their implicit model (despite their rhetoric), Africans found that political equality could be acquired at a much lower price than that of economic competitiveness. And so, on multiple fronts they demanded, and were usually given, the inexpensive version of equality.

A pessimistic perspective on African development and its relationships with the rest of the world comes from the pen of Henry Louis Gates, an African-American scholar writing about his work at a hospital two decades earlier in Tanzania as a member of the Peace Corps:

> To my surprise and dismay, I found myself—despite myself—longing for the order and resources that the missionaries had brought to the Wagogo [people] in earlier years. Their residences, as well as the hospital buildings, were in great disrepair. The standard of living, and the villagers' life expectancy, had not been raised one jot over the past two decades. Looking around the village, I realized that even if the West stood still for a thousand years, my friends in Killimatinde would never catch up. And the West, of course, will never stand still.[7]

NOTES

1. See UNDP for detailed data on this and related topics.

2. President Mobutu decreed, for example, that his countrymen should abandon their European names in favor of "authentic" Zaïrian ones; he became Mobutu Sese Seko instead of Joseph Desirée. "Western" dress was replaced with

the *abacost (à bas le costume*—"down with the costume") for men and the *pagne* for women. Expatriate businesses were transferred arbitrarily to Zaïrians, at great cost in lost productivity, and control of education was wrested from the church in order to Africanize the learning process.

3. One author describes the "African personality as a dialogue of two selves," the present *ego* and the ubiquitous array of ancestors.

4. There is, of course, the paradox of those Westerners who proclaim spiritual values (e.g., some missionaries) but who also exhibit extreme materialism.

5. Julius Jeppe, "Cultural Dimensions of Development Policy Management in the New South Africa," *DPMN Bulletin* 2 (August 1994): 8.

6. *Negritude* was revived in the 1970s with the Festival of African Culture in Nigeria which was to become a regular event. That did not come to pass.

7. "Going Back," *The New Republic*, 16 June 1997, p. 22.

CHAPTER 8

Dilemmas of Development

Achieving independence is only one part of the battle for national self-control. Once independence is achieved, political leaders must set about the business of running a country, which is much easier to talk about than to do. Below we discuss some of the more salient issues which confronted virtually all African leaders when independence was gained. Of course, not all dilemmas are equally applicable to all states, nor are all equally significant. However,

Despite massive injections of foreign capital, poverty is a persistent reality in Africa. Here, an Islamic auto dealer in Mafeking, South Africa, is observing one of the fundamental tenets of Islam by distributing food to the poor.

they represent categories of issues which beset newly independent, generally poor states with no tradition of dealing with the
economic and political challenges of sovereignty.

These issues are couched as challenges to individual leaders, because the governance of most of the new states of Africa
was very much personalized. Uniparty politics, heroic revolutionary leaders, and a traditional propensity to tolerate authority,
regardless of the structure proclaimed or even enshrined in a document, made the business of running the country very much
attributable to a single individual.

These thirteen specific challenges are addressed to a hypothetical leader, and their meaning and implications are discussed,
but no response or solution is offered. There was, in fact, a wide
variety of responses, and nonresponses, and thinking about these
is an effective way to "understand Africa." So I invite *you* to think,
"How does a leader . . ?"

- **How does a leader minimize internal conflicts:
  urban-rural, traditional-modern, interethnic?**

All modern societies can record gaps between urban and
rural portions of their populations, but this gap is perhaps greater
in Africa than elsewhere. The city—and there generally is only one
large city in an African state—has the university, the tertiary care
hospital, the airport, the secretarial school, the stores that provide
the "stuff" of modern life, and on and on. The rural area may
offer little more than villages with incredibly understocked shops[1]
and rudimentary infrastructure, perhaps a well, a semblance of a
school, and some sort of medical facility.

Malawian village shops might contain two (perhaps three)
versions of Carlsberg beer because of a large and aggressive brew-
ing operation, several Coca-Cola products (for the same reason),
and bags of "creamed maize" (corn which has been degermed
and hulled and then milled into a very smooth flour for the staple
dish of the area, *nsima*). There might be a few boxes or cans of

detergent, salt, cooking oil, kerosene (for cooking-stoves and lanterns in the absence of electricity), perhaps bread, and wheat flour. Vendors in front of the shop might sell cassava, in-season fruits and vegetables (pineapple, banana, guava, mangoes, papaya, tomatoes, potatoes, green beans, eggplant, corn, herbs, a few spices), and that may well be it.

Life in the city certainly offers more variety if one can afford to take advantage of it. But the traditional-modern conflict is much more deep-seated than mere material differences suggest. Consequently, it is more difficult to deal with. The American cliché, "You can't teach an old dog new tricks," does not begin to capture the challenge of bringing someone across the metaphorical centuries from rural Africa to cope successfully with a modern city—should one even think that such an effort is legitimate.[2] This is not to say that such cultural travel does not happen every day. From a moralistic perspective, the choice about whether to embark on such a journey should remain with the individual involved and not with some planner in an office in "government central." The attractions of the city too often overwhelm all other considerations, and people are attracted to the morass of urban life with little or no preparation for its challenges and no linkages to sustain their social identity.

African villagers may have no more than a few dollars (in their own currency, of course) pass through their hands in the course of a year. Their food is home grown or acquired through bartering. A few seasonings (particularly salt and sugar) and a few clothes may be all they purchase. If they are lucky, perhaps they will acquire a radio or a bicycle or a paraffin (kerosene) lamp or stove. They do not participate in commerce in the Western sense, and their view of the world is very much other-worldly—e.g., pre-Newtonian in terms of science. Most are nonliterate.[3]

The reinforcing circumstances which impede development in much of Africa consist of more than aspects of poverty. Some are universal problems—e.g., ethnicity and its political ramifications. Africans are not *sui generis* when it comes to political problems. As a matter of fact, as they have achieved limited development, their capacity to engage in disruptive activities has increased.

Interethnic conflict is omnipresent in today's world. Witness Northern Ireland, Rwanda, Yugoslavia, Israel. Each of these is a case of, if not explicitly "interethnic" conflict, surely "intergroup" conflict between "some" and the "others." Its pervasiveness suggests how easy such hostility is to induce and suggests likewise how difficult it is to resolve. Africa, with its thousand or so ethnic groups, is ripe for such disputes. Look at the tragic African examples: Zulus in South Africa taking out after Xhosa, Sotho, and others; Moslems in Egypt attacking Copts; Hutus and Tutsis in Rwanda and Burundi slaughtering one another; or various Nigerian groups and the Ibo warring with one another. The boundaries created at the Berlin Conference took no note of ethnicity, so there are multiple ethnicities in virtually every African state, and ethnic groups are likewise separated by borders. The good news is that, given these myriad groups, for most of the continent there are only three choices: learn to live with multiethnicity, be consigned to microstates so small as to be unsustainable, or live with perpetual conflict. President Mandela of South Africa confronted this dilemma early in his life: Reporting on the marriage of friends of different tribes, he said that this "began to undermine my parochialism and loosen the hold of the tribalism that still imprisoned me" (p. 45).

While some groups have been able to live together peaceably, all that is required to destroy a placid situation is a demagogue who arouses chauvinistic sentiments (e.g., the battles following the collapse of Yugoslavia, the CIA-supported Inkhata Freedom Movement in South Africa), especially if one group has a grievance that can easily be blamed on others.[4] When there is a dearth of distractions—especially in the absence of satisfying economic development—the opportunity for ethnic hostility is maximized—and this has regularly been the case in postindependence Africa.

One ominous legacy of internal conflict is land mines

which are a standard item in civil conflict. The United Nations has highlighted these mines as a major impediment to development worldwide. In Angola alone, it is estimated that twenty million land mines remain after a generation of internal conflict. Since their placement was not mapped, removal is both dangerous and costly, requiring sophisticated training and equipment. Until removal is completed, however, one of the major medical problems such states confront is the need for prostheses to replace limbs blown off innocent victims. This is one of many opportunity costs imposed by military expenditures: resources that could otherwise be devoted to human development issues. In this case, however, the expenditures do not take the form of a benign rusting tank or artillery piece; those are essentially harmless. The lethal capacity of mines remains long after their tactical use has been obviated, and they generally "attack" individuals who are the least involved—e.g., farmers or children.

- **How does a leader obtain the resources to satisfy material needs without a tax base and without making crippling external commitments in exchange for funds?**

Just as one cannot "get blood from a turnip," one cannot extract government income from a society which is already poor, which holds a residual antipathy to government, and which engages largely in informal economic activity. It has become axiomatic that avenues to modernization have been largely the province of IGOs, NGOs, and occasionally private businesses. (See table 8.1.) But, as many states have learned, external assistance comes at a price: interference in decision making, dependency, lack of control in placing resources, and political demands.

During the Cold War the majority of external funding came through channels subject to overt political pressure, and a given state's share was very much a function of the prevailing political climate of the time. In more recent years, pressure for "structural

TABLE 8.1

Central Government Revenues*

State	1 Revenue from Income Taxes—Percent, 1987	2 Non-tax Revenue Percent, 1987	3 Total Revenue as Percent GNP	4 Current account Balance: Percent GDP 1987
Botswana	38.1	47.2	75.2	7.5
Burkina Faso	20.6	10.5	15.3	0.8
Chad	20.8	11.6	5.7	-4.5
Gabon	44.2	31.2	47.1	1.9
Ghana	21.5	10.6	14.5	-5.1
Kenya	30.4	10.9	20.8	-0.8
Lesotho	11.1	10.5	22	14.1
Liberia	34.1	4.4	17	—

Malawi	35.5	18.2	22.6	-34.9
Mali	8.2	10.1	15.1	-8.9
Nigeria	39.9	62.9	18.5	9.7
Sierra Leone	28	5.6	6.5	-9.6
South Africa	52.7	8.6	29.2	-1.6
Tanzania	25.8	5.1	16.3	-15.8
Togo	35.7	22.2	31.8	-6.1
Uganda	5.5	0	9.3	-8.2
Zaire	29.9	15.2	16.3	—
Zambia	23.5	3	24.4	—
Zimbabwe	42.8	16.6	12.9	-2.1

Sources: World Bank, *World Development Report 1989*; pp. 186–187.

*Of the nineteen African states for which there are data, the average revenue from income taxes (column 1) is under 30 percent. Non-tax revenue (column 2) averages sixteen percent. With the impoverished underlying economies, it is difficult for African leaders to undertake projects which require resources that cannot be generated from within the system.

adjustment" has been the order of the day (see Box 2.9). Put simply, one of the political functions of a developing system was seeing to the well-being of those who presented the greatest threat to that system. Often those people were residents of the capital city—civil servants, opinion leaders, university students, and the affluent. Each group in its own way could make life difficult for the government.

One direct way to placate these groups was through subsidies for basic needs—transportation, staple food, and education for their children. This was the general pattern and it was usually a significant item in the strapped budgets of African states. This policy, however, had the unfortunate unintended consequence of discouraging food production. Consider: If the *real* cost of a loaf of bread, for example, is 100, but the government decides to set (or maintain) the price at 20, the difference of 80 must be made up either in a subsidy or in lower profits to the farmers and bakers. If food prices are lower, farmers will switch from wheat to tobacco or groundnuts or whatever can be sold in the open market to recover their real costs and garner a profit. Food will have to be purchased by the state on the open market. When this situation arises among several states, there is increased competition in the international marketplace for basic foodstuffs. Meanwhile, all the relevant populations are growing geometrically.

As time passes, the subsidy gap usually grows because the costs of inputs such as fertilizer, seeds, and tractors increase, along with the population, continually raising the cost of the government subsidy. As one of the several substantial and important costs of government, this subsidy is a crucial part of the budget. A government which decides to recover the real cost of the bread and raise the price from 20 to 100 faces great unhappiness. Under IMF pressure Tunisia and Zambia did this and violence erupted. Nonetheless, if the government is to balance its budget, this is one area in which it can recover costs and at the same time make farming more attractive: by raising returns to growers. This assumes, of course, that the growers are smallholders and not industrial farms. International lending institutions, under pressure especially from the United States and Britain, have increasingly insisted on open markets and on charging real prices for all commodities as conditions for making or renewing loans. It is regularly and fairly logically argued that structural adjustment, while certainly reallocating government funds and increasing the incentive for farmers, also raises the cost of survival in a society. Hence, it is inflationary, and workers demand more in order to pay more for the same product. This puts the poorest at a disadvantage while benefiting the international financial system and financial institutions in the West. Looking at structural adjustment in another way, during most of the 1980s, the net flow of capital to developing countries turned negative; that is they were required to return more in loan repayments to lenders than they received in cash transfers as development assistance and refinanced loans.

Resistance, however, subjects the state to cash shortfalls which wreak difficulties on all segments of the population, no matter which way things go. As with controlled economies, so it is with uncontrolled economies: The frailties of human nature introduce problems which only rational policy fairly enforced can control. At present, the policy pendulum has swung away from controlled economies and in the direction of totally free markets through structural adjustment. In a few years, it will be due for readjustment again.

- **How does a leader approach the problem of population excess when religion, and economic and social conditions reject population control?**

The arguments of the Roman Catholic Church against birth control are well known. Less well known are other, more subtle factors which impede population control efforts. For example, it is axiomatic that in a subsistence society the more hands available to work in the field, the better. And since subsistence farming characterizes most of rural Africa, this is a consideration. In affluent Western societies, children are a distinct economic liability. The tens of thousands of dollars required to pay for a middle-class infant to become a self-sufficient adult serve as a deterrent to large families. The opposite phenomenon is found in much of Africa.

Another set of contrasts is seen in social welfare: Affluent Western societies provide for those who are no longer able to work (e.g., social security in the United States). But in Africa, social welfare programs, if they exist at all, generally do not include the elderly, so there is a logical desire to have a large family in the hope that at least one child will do well enough to support the parents in their old age.[5]

Also, infant mortality, which ranges from 50 per 1,000 in South Africa to 191 in Niger, can prompt parents to have multiple children in hope of a few surviving. When one factors in *child* mortality as well, the incentive to have more children increases. The uncertainties of life on the edge of starvation induce behaviors that residents of the affluent West cannot readily comprehend.

- **How does a leader assure adequate political allegiance while fostering openness?**

This dilemma is predicated on the assumption that an open society is desirable and possible in Africa. It depends, of course, on the definition of "adequate." Setting that aside for the moment, the question of balance on the continuum from open to closed societies is regularly presented. For example, preliterate people must have civic consciousness inculcated through such practices as placing photographs of the "leader" in public places (post offices, schools, transportation terminals). Unless this is done with care, it can easily lead to adulation that verges on—or becomes—religious devotion.[6] This tends to silence criticism, impede policy discussion, render disagreement suspicious, and lead to imposition of authoritarian regimes. How many African political opponents have been permanently silenced is unknowable, but their numbers include rogues and rascals and bishops, physicians, and students.

There is a legitimate question about how "open" a developing system can be on a sustainable basis. The tradition of "chiefs" has created an acquiescence to authoritarianism. In a tribal context a consultative process may be built in, but when "chiefdom" is imposed over millions of people and thousands of square kilometers, the possibility of genuine consultation falls by the board.[7]

An open and participatory system—the current "fad" of democracy—requires behavior which is generally alien to new African states: tolerance of differing opinions, acceptance of defeat in an election, meritocratic resolution of questions, meritocratic hiring of government employees, open and free flow of information (transparency, in current jargon). While some traditions easily accommodate these principles, others do not; and as the complexity of modern systems grows, the challenge of communicating policy options to a public that participates in political decisions becomes increasingly difficult. Indeed, Western societies themselves are seeing alienation and hostility among their own citizens in the postindustrial age.

- **How does a leader procure technical expertise for his system while keeping the revolution of rising expectations under control?**

The revolution of rising expectations (see Box 3.7) is the process in which individuals, groups, or entire societies continually increase their material expectations as they grow more aware of possibilities and more able to approximate acquiring them. For example, once electricity arrives at a location, why should we not have a television, a refrigerator, a fan? Where there is no electricity, those without televisions, etc., would not be disappointed, because those other modern "goodies" would not be attainable. Once the prerequisites are obtained, people become unhappy about what they cannot have, and revolutionary thoughts are more likely to be entertained.

Every introduction of technology suggests the possibility of alternative applications; the tractor that increases the farmer's grain yield may also provide transportation into town for shopping or entertainment. It is said in Malawi, for example, that ambulances are used for transporting hospital staff to and from work and shopping as much as for bringing patients to the hospital or clinic.[8]

This situation is analogous to the invention of dynamite: Dynamite can be utilized for good or ill. It has no inherent value in and of itself; only the ends to which it is put can be valued. So it is with introducing change: All kinds of change may be deemed desirable, but every change has the potential for both positive and negative consequences for the development process. Any change can produce unintended consequences. Even if a change is clearly desirable, it is not possible to manage the change process so that only "good" changes are introduced. Indeed, who would be empowered to determine what is "good"? One can only hope that the general balance of resources remains positive, and that popular aspirations do not get out of control.

- **How does a leader prepare to deal with external threats while keeping the military focused on its domestic role?**

It is said that "In the kingdom of the blind, the one-eyed man is king." It is relative, not absolute, advantage that determines superiority. So it is with the military in African states; it may not be objectively powerful, but it is well ahead of whatever institution or organization is in second place. On the premise that every self-respecting state must have an army, individuals may acquire the capacity for superior force, but lack the commitment of the military to the principles and/or protection of the sitting government. Or in some cases to the principles and goals of the opposition. If the differences between the preferences of those with the guns and those with the laws is too great, the system is ripe for a military coup. If those preferences are generally in accord, the system may become tyrannical.

External threats are often reciprocal, regardless of absolute levels of capability: State A is arming, which leads State B to respond. This worries State A, which raises its level of armaments, and so on. Unless there is a strong popular commitment to the system rather than to a given individual or specific issue, the military can undo the best-laid plans of any government, as it has in myriad instances in Nigeria, Benin, the Central African Republic, Sierra Leone, Rwanda, and elsewhere.

Table 8.2 indicates two dimensions of development in the realm of arms: the portion of budgets spent on the military and arms transfers to African states. For example, over a third of Ethiopia's imports in 1985 and over a quarter of Angola's were arms. At the same time, Ethiopia ranked 156 out of 157 states in per-capita income. Column 3 in table 8.2 is a measure of priorities, in this case arms versus health and education.

- **How does a leader economize while providing the trappings of sovereignty?**

This may not seem the most pressing of problems, but very small matters acquire great importance when a system is fragile. Symbolism is important in establishing the credibility of a new regime. How many limousines are required for the president to be taken seriously? Or to be seen as equal in prestige to European leaders? How many residences are sufficient for the president's entertaining of foreign diplomats and corporate CEOs? Should he have an airplane? . . . a fleet?

President Nyerere of Tanzania received a salary of US$6,000 in the 1970s, and Tanzanian government officials were forbidden to own property other than their homes. He was comfortable with his standing—and it was indeed impressive. But

TABLE 8.2

Military Expenditures

State	1 Military Expenditures per Capita, 1984 (1983 dollars)	2 Arms Imports as Percent of Total Imports 1985	3 Military Expenditure (as Percent of Health and Education) 1990–1991
Angola	—	25.9	208
Benin	7	—	—
Botswana	25	0	22
Burkina Faso	4	9.5	30
Burundi	8	2.6	42
Cameroon	14	6.3	48
CAR	—	0	33
Chad	2	23.4*	74
Congo	31	3.2	37
Ethiopia	10	39.3	19
Gabon	72	14.8	51
Ghana	28	1.7	12
Kenya	10	0.3	24
Lesotho	37	0	48
Liberia	10	3.1	—
Madagascar	7	5.7	37
Malawi	3	1.7	24
Mali	3	1.7	53
Niger	2	—	11
Nigeria	12	4.4	—
Senegal	9	0	33
Sierra Leone	2	0	23
Somalia	14	26.8	—
South Africa	108	0	41
Sudan	6	5.2	44
Swaziland	16	0	11
Tanzania	10	2	77
Togo	6	5.2	39
Uganda	5	1.3	18
Zaire	3	2.5	71
Zambia	31	1.5	63
Zimbabwe	44	5.3	66

Source: *U.S. Arms Control and Disarmament Agency, World Military Expenditures and Arms Transfers 1986; UNDP Human Development Report 1998, p. 170.*

*Anomalous—substantially higher than other recent years.

many leaders do not feel so secure that they can be comfortable with such restraint. And, of course, when leaders visit abroad and see Buckingham Palace or the Elysée Palace, they quickly forget the difference in age, tradition, and resources between their thirty-year-old state with a per capita gross domestic product of $500[9] and Britain or France.

- **How does a leader afford to send knowledgeable but undertrained bureaucrats for further training, risking that they will become threats to his government or be "brain-drained" to a richer locale?**

Despite the British tradition of introducing universities, at independence most African states lacked institutions of higher education. They sorely needed engineers, teachers, physicians, lawyers, and public administrators. The only way to bridge the gap in a tolerable amount of time was to seek education outside the continent (since South Africa was an unacceptable option). Thus, hundreds of Africans—then and now—left home to seek additional training abroad. From the British colonies, people often went to Britain, Canada, or the United States; from Francophone Africa they traveled to France.

What many discovered was:

1. They became so liberated from tradition (see Mandela's early chapters) that they could not return home and fit into the more constraining or repressive culture, and they would not be welcome in their new incarnations.
2. They could marry a citizen and gain European or North American citizenship.
3. Even working at the bottom of the pay scale in an industrial economy would put them ahead of where they would be at home. For these reasons, many who went abroad for education never returned. Virtually any large professional enterprise in the United States is populated

with its share of Africans (not to mention Asians, Latin Americans, and Eastern Europeans) who can be considered part of the brain drain. The problem is so severe that many U.S. institutions have adopted policies requiring students to return home upon completion of their education, thus contributing to the society which initially invested in their becoming a professional.[10]

If one becomes too adamant on this issue, there will be a great loss to industrial countries' education—i.e., the absence of African faculty or students will impoverish university learning in the West, and there will be a reduction in the number of engineers, lawyers, or dentists. Until the rewards professionals can expect in Africa approximate those they can reap in the West (at least in "purchasing power parity"—the ability to acquire similar goods regardless of their price in a particular currency—and until the quality of life is less disparate, the brain drain will continue.

- **How does a leader manage this dilemma: Improving the health of the people may lead to a famine if food production is not increased, but population can be reduced by letting people suffer and die.**

This is perhaps the key issue in development, because development is relative, not absolute. The resources of any African state could support a population of five hundred or one thousand people (or even a larger number) at a high level of comfort and security. Deprivation and problems arise when a given quantity of available resources is stretched among too many people. Regrettably, the overwhelming needs of many states— whether in political or economic terms—resulted in shortsighted behavior by leaders. One minister of agriculture said: "The priority of the Republic of Congo is development for its people. If this necessitates the destruction of the forests of the country, it will be done" (U.S. Representative E. Clay Shaw, before Africa Subcommittee hearing, 19 March 1997).

One reason why population has exploded, of course, is improved health care and hygiene. To teach people to wash their hands before eating imposes next to zero cost on the system, but it may prolong average life by a measurable amount of time. Those individuals will have to eat, and they may or may not be economically productive. Smallpox inoculations are inexpensive, and they clearly save lives. Of course, saving lives is an unarguable policy objective. But once a life is saved, there is no corollary provision for meeting the needs of individuals whose lives have been lengthened. They will need jobs, food, shelter, and clothing.

Health and hygiene have improved for Africans (at least till the onset of the AIDS pandemic) more than any other conditions. As a consequence of a World Health Organization decision, for example, smallpox has been eradicated not only from Africa, but from the face of the earth. Dysentery, gonorrhea, leprosy, and other maladies of the poor and malnourished have responded to relatively inexpensive modern medicines. Many lives have been saved, and the survivors have the potential to become economically productive. The sad fact is, however, that not everyone who reaches adulthood has the opportunity to make a meaningful contribution to society. Food problems regularly attend the diminution of disease, and disastrous environmental degradation follows. No one can argue for suspending health education or health care; but what one can—and must, vehemently—argue for is population control, family planning. The number of children born must be curtailed, despite the fact that this conflicts head-on with the positions of the Roman Catholic Church and Islam which are influential in a number of African states. When infant mortality drops from 220 per thousand to 80 and there is no corollary increase in resources, compensatory steps must be taken. Short of infanticide or murder, there is no other option but limiting population growth.

Consequences of overpopulation affect every aspect of life. To offer a few illustrations:

- Schools become overcrowded and must be augmented.
- Marginal farmland is brought under cultivation, resulting

in lowered production, soil erosion, increased need for fertilizer, polluted water, and declining incomes.

- Transportation systems become overburdened.
- Life itself loses some of its value when people are everywhere scrambling for survival.

We are discussing more than increased marginal costs. One additional student in a school makes little difference, but a doubling of the school's population can be catastrophic without a commensurate increase of resources. There is no panacea, but if one principal step could be taken to bring a better life to most African states, shrinking the population would be it.[11] Then one could get on with improving the health of the remaining citizens with less fear of future disasters.

- **How does a leader induce saving for capital accumulation while potential savers witness ever-increasing consumer opportunities?**

It is difficult—no, it is probably impossible—for the average American reader to grasp the marginality of many Africans' existence. The chap who peddles pineapples door to door could not have made more than a dollar or two a day, maybe $350 per year if all went well. That is a subsistence existence; there is no extra money for clothes, school fees, medicine, emergencies, luxuries, or saving.

Capital accumulation is necessary to provide for investment in capital equipment, for example. But if no one can save, then no one can borrow. Consequently, there can be no large-scale development without resources from outside. This leaves the recipients beholden to the providers—either governments or private interests—neither of which is primarily interested in the well-being of the African state, but in its own interests.

At the same time, while one might be able to eke out an existence if that $350 a year could somehow be raised to $355 or

$455 or $1,055, the increase would almost certainly be seen as discretionary income and would be consumed instead of deposited in a savings account. After years of deprivation and scrambling to better one's situation, pent up consumer need and desire, regardless of culture, will cause people to consume large increases in income before they think of saving. Furthermore, as one's income increases, one's consumption moves up the economic scale: Instead of eating grain or root porridge, a staple of African rural diets, one can use a few extra coins to eat meat or fish occasionally. A substantial increase can be consumed in the buying of soft drinks, canned goods, paper towels, candy, or whatever may be perceived as adding status to one's image.

There are ways to encourage savings, of course—by compulsion or by inducement. A portion of income, at least for those who work in the formal sector, could be appropriated by the government and put into controlled savings. This obviously would not be a popular or even tolerable arrangement in many places, and I know of no place in Africa where it has occurred. Inducement, on the other hand, is more palatable, but essentially unaffordable. If one were offered exorbitant interest rates on savings (perhaps 40 percent) people might defer consumption in favor of savings. But the distortion of the marketplace that 40 percent interest on savings would produce makes the cure worse than the disease. In this age of internationally mobile capital, the only way to protect such a situation would be through harsh controls, imposing yet another unbearable cost on the system.

Table 8.3 reinforces other data indicating the very slow growth of nonagricultural sectors in most African economies. Table 6.2 illustrates hypothetical growth rates and suggests the difficulties a poor states faces when competing in a world of relatively rich states growing at similar or faster rates. Table 8.3 indicates *actual* growth over the decade of the 1980s. There is little hope of African states attaining an economic level comparable to that of the richer states without dramatic and convulsive economic transformations.

TABLE 8.3
Sectoral Production Growth (average annual growth, 1980–1987)

	1	2	3	4	5	6	7
	GDP	Agriculture	Industry	Manufacturing	Services	Population Growth Rate*	Natural Increase Rate†
Angola	—	—	—	—	—	2.7	2.7
Benin	2.8	2.5	8.3	4.6	1.3	2.8	3.3
Botswana	13.0	−7.8	19.2	4.5	9.5	3.3	1.1
Burkina Faso	5.6	6.1	3.9	—	5.8	2.7	2.9
Burundi	2.6	1.7	4.9	6.6	3.5	2.2	2.4
Cameroon	7.0	2.4	11.0	8.5	6.9	2.8	2.8
CAR	2.0	2.4	2.2	0.3	1.6	2.3	2.2
Chad	5.1	2.6	10.0	8.5	6.3	2.2	2.7
Congo	5.5	1.5	10.9	9.7	−1.9	2.9	2.2
Cote d'Ivoire	2.2	1.6	−2.4	8.2	4.2	3.7	2.6
Djibouti	—	—	—	—	—	5.8	2.7
Eritrea	—	—	—	—	—	2.2	3.0
Ethiopia	0.9	−2.1	3.8	3.8	3.5	2.7	2.3
Gabon	0.6	—	—	—	—	—	1.5
Gambia	—	—	—	—	—	3.6	3.0
Ghana	1.4	0.0	0.1	1.3	4.2	2.8	2.2
Guinea	—	—	—	—	—	2.6	2.4

Guinea-Bissau	—	—	—	—	—	2.9	2.3
Kenya	3.8	3.4	3.0	4.3	4.4	3.5	1.7
Lesotho	2.3	0.4	0.4	12.9	4.0	2.6	1.9
Madagascar	0.3	2.2	-2.0	—	-0.5	3.1	2.8
Malawi	2.6	2.5	1.9	—	3.0	3.1	1.4
Mali	3.4	0.3	9.8	—	5.9	2.8	3.1
Mozambique	-2.6	-11.1	-8.4	—	6.2	2.5	2.6
Namibia	—	—	—	—	—	2.7	1.6
Niger	-1.9	2.8	-4.3	—	-8.0	—	3.0
Nigeria	-1.7	0.6	-4.4	-2.1	-0.3	2.9	2.9
Senegal	3.3	4.2	4.3	4.3	2.4	2.8	3.3
Sierra Leone	0.7	1.6	-2.3	0.6	1.3	1.9	2.9
South Africa	1.0	0.3	-0.1	-0.5	2.3	2.5	1.4
Sudan	—	—	—	—	—	2.7	2.9
Swaziland	—	—	—	—	—	2.9	2.0
Tanzania	1.7	3.8	-2.4	-3.5	0.8	3.2	2.4
Togo	-0.5	0.8	-1.6	—	-0.7	2.9	3.5
Uganda	0.4	-0.5	1.4	-0.9	3.0	2.8	2.3
Zaire	1.6	3.2	3.6	0.6	-1.2	3.3	3.2
Zambia	-0.1	3.2	-0.7	0.8	-0.6	2.7	—
Zimbabwe	2.4	2.3	1.4	1.8	3.3	3.1	—

From: United Nations Development Program, Human Development Report 1998, (*) and (†) USAID, *World Population Profile 1998.*

• How can a program of sustainable development be devised to protect future development possibility while at the same time satisfying the pressing demands of an eager populace?

Throughout the developing world—in Africa, Latin America, and Asia—we see repeated disasters as fragile resources are overused to satisfy immediate needs with little or no attention to conservation. Probably the most pervasive example is overcutting of forests for timber and for firewood. One essential for health (and for flavor) is *cooking* food, which requires concentrated heat. This can conceivably be produced by solar ovens, but in actuality it generally comes from the burning of wood (or charcoal, which produces the same effect).

From whatever source, economic data for Africa are depressing. Table 8.4 presents prices for 24 of these commodities on which Africa depends for foreign earnings. Over a twenty-year period, prices for 14 of these commodities have declined in absolute terms. During this same period, prices for goods that Africa imports—primarily manufactured products—have risen.

Evidence shows, as in table 5.2, that people have to work harder and harder to obtain heat whether that means spending more time walking to and gathering wood or paying higher prices to wood and charcoal vendors. While the primary products produced by most Africans have lost or gained little in value, the manufactured products that they desire have increased in cost and value over this same period. As forests are depleted, people settle in greater and greater concentrations, exacerbating the problem geometrically. Conservation, however sensible in the long run, is almost invariably seen as unnecessary or undesirable in the short run. Witness the difficulties encountered in adopting conservation measures in the "civilized" West where there is supposedly sufficient sophistication to comprehend the opportunity costs of wasteful resource consumption. Sustainable development is not unlike AIDS prevention: Both require that those whose behaviors

TABLE 8.4
Commodity Prices: Average Annual Growth Rate, 1960–1980 (%)

Copper	−5.5
Iron Ore	−8.5
Bauxite	3.9
Phosphate rock	−0.2
Manganese ore	−6.4
Zinc	−0.7
Tin	4.3
Lead	1.6
Coffee	2.3
Cocoa	5.5
Sugar	−2.5
Tea	−3.4
Groundnuts	−1.7
Groundnut Oil	−1.6
Beef	1.5
Palm Oil	−2.0
Bananas	−4.0
Maize	0.2
Timber	0.7
Cotton	−1.0
Tobacco	0.1
Rubber	−2.3
Hides, skins	0
Sisal	−2.8

Source: World Bank, *Accelerated Development in Sub-Saharan Africa*, p. 157.

are being changed understand that consequences of today's behavior reach into some indefinite future.

A major aspect of the challenge is weighing political and economic decisions in the short run. Industrial development, which is intricately tied to the political elite, is seldom attentive to sustainable development. Decisions are generally made far from the point of their impact, so unwise choices carry no immediate penalty.

- **How does a leader further African unity while protecting national interests vis-à-vis neighboring states?**

Lip service to African unity has been paid by virtually every African leader for thirty years. In theory, it is a good idea. In practice, however, unity has not been meaningfully achieved anywhere on the continent, with the single exception of Tanganyika's union with Zanzibar (and that has not been problem-free). The unions of Senegal and Gambia, Egypt and Libya (and Syria), or the East African Community have all failed as of this writing.

The requirements for successful unions are such that no region of Africa presents an ideal setting. Fundamental requirements should include most, if not all, of the following:

1. Political will
2. Complementary economies
3. Popular acceptance
4. The perception of tolerable costs, especially on the part of richer partners
5. Common history, heritage, and values
6. Geographic contiguity
7. Visible and fearsome external threat
8. Effective external pressure[12]

Conditions one and two are particularly important, and it is just these two that are most lacking in Africa. The next two can be manipulated by most governments if the arrangement proves useful. The Anglophone and Francophone colonies do share some commonalities, but these are offset by great ethnic diversity. Geographic contiguity can be arranged, except that the infrastructure, as mentioned elsewhere, was not originally developed to favor integrating neighboring economies. External threats and pressure are certainly different in the post-Cold War era, but a new array of threats is looming—e.g., environmental degradation, AIDS, poverty, infrastructure deterioration. All these would be susceptible to regional solutions, or at least improvements.

The real challenge for most leaders lies in functionally defining interests and threats. There is little question that regionalism could benefit most African states. South Africa or Zaire might be exceptions since both are large and potentially very wealthy, but even they could benefit from merged markets, etc. Unfortunately, African leaders have not taken the risks to identify and articulate multinational interests. Their regimes have too often been threatened, internally or externally, and they have used neighboring states as enemies in order to rally their own populace. That precluded reaching out and across borders for the larger common good.

- **How does a leader reconcile the European background prevalent in most colonies with the economically desirable austerity of traditional society?**

We have already mentioned that African states became immediate actors on the international stage at the time of independence. They were associating and even competing with large, rich, old states in both diplomatic arenas and in infrastructure development. Such trappings of state as international airports and airlines, universities, military uniforms and equipment, embassy staffing, and so on were constantly on display.

Some, but not all, of the costs were borne by the international community—e.g., the former colonial metropoles or the Cold War combatants—and outsiders did not pay the costs of sustaining such activity after the initial investment. Furthermore, the superficial appearance of successful competition was often belied by underlying inadequacies. While in graduate school in Washington, D.C., this author visited most African embassies to collect their then-current constitutions for use in a research project. In most cases, the effort was unsuccessful; they did not have copies of their *new* governments' constitutions. (Imagine visiting a European embassy and not finding a copy of that state's constitution!) And so the trappings of a "real" state were acquired, but they were not sustainable without the substance.

In the process of development, a wide range of choices must be made and priorities established. U.N. Human Development data demonstrate the vast differences in priorities reflected in outcomes of similarly-positioned states. (The comparison is between human development outcomes in states with similar GNPs per capita; not all are African.)

What is apparent from these figures, regardless of whether the states are African, is that some options are available to states at any given level of development. In each of the non-African cases, different choices were made, as reflected in the outcomes in these data (see table 8.5). Collectively, the citizens of Sri Lanka, Ecuador, and Chile, while at different levels of development, are all better off from a human development perspective than similarly poor (or rich) African states. Remarkably, both Sri Lanka and Ecuador rank above South Africa in HDI value despite their much lower GNPs per capita. This demonstrates clearly that it is not absolute resources but their deployment that makes the greatest difference in achieving human betterment. Put differently, with a given array of resources, a state can choose to increase literacy, lower infant mortality, and in general improve the lives of its citizens; or it can opt for military training instead of medical training or "perks" for cabinet ministers instead of education. For example, in the first comparison: Guinea has a life expectancy of 44 years; Sri Lanka, 71. In the Congo and Ecuador the corresponding data are 59 and 87. The best one can conclude from this is that even poor states are not without choices; the worst is that relatively minor choices have exponential impact on systems.

TABLE 8.5

Development Priorities as Seen in Outcomes, 1990s

Country	GNP p.c. (US$)	HDI Value	Life Expectancy	Adult Literacy	Infant Mortality per 1,000	Age at First Marriage	Food Production on 1979–1981 = 100
GNP per capita, $400–$500							
Sr Lanka	500	0.665	71.2	89	24	24.4	90
Guinea	500	0.191	43.9	27	135	16.0	90
GNP per capita, $1,000–$1,100							
Ecuador	1,010	0.718	66.2	87	58	21.1	115
Congo	1,040	0.461	51.7	59	83	21.9	92
GNP per capita, $2,300–$2,600							
Chile	2,360	0.848	71.9	94	17	23.4	117
South Africa	2,540	0.650	62.2	80	53	26.1	82

Data from: United Nations, *Human Development Report 1994*, pp. 15, 144, 154.

One development issue that cannot be prepared for but has had profound impact on specific regions in Africa is refugees. When thousands or millions flee from some catastrophe to the ostensible safety of another state, disruptions of several kinds occur; and all detract from orderly progress toward further development. Looking at the numbers in table 8.6 suggests that huge migrations have imposed great costs. Every refugee represents some number of deaths, destruction of home and crops, potential for disease or crime, and instability. Every individual who is displaced represents crops not planted and not harvested, family responsibilities not attended to, social ties severed, and other costs imposed upon a system.

While this enumeration can be extended, it is indicative of the wide and deep array of problems, choices, and policy options which confronted African leaders. Many of these leaders were not secure in their positions and could afford no risks, nor did they have the political capital to expend in selling their populations on courses of action contrary to popular expectations. Generally, expectations were set not by cautious and thoughtful leaders, but by media and rhetoricians seeking political gain or by external sources over which the government had no control.

Every one of these issues was implicitly answered time and again in every state; they are the "stuff" of which public policy is made. If one were to construct a report card for each state on these eleven issues, the rare state would receive a high grade. Such

TABLE 8.6
Numbers of Refugees

	Refugees—1992
Mozambique	4,720,000
Somalia	870,000
Ethiopia	840,000
Liberia	670,000
Angola	400,000

Source: *Human Development Report 1994.*

an estimate may seem harsh, but it is not a value judgment so much as a policy assessment. The value judgment would come only after one assessed the motives and aspirations of the citizens of the various states in relationship to what their leaders told them and the consonance between these two phenomena.

Consider the origins of the United States. While the issues were different, they were of similar import when this country had its beginnings. It is instructive to recall that the Articles of Confederation, the basic document of government for our first decade, did not in the final analysis prove adequate to the task. This was less a failure of specific individuals than of a system that was inappropriate. Nonetheless, the system of governance for the world's most successful revolutionary system failed in its first decade. It did not do so in front of television cameras, however, and few people in the rest of the world knew or cared. Not so with Africa; much of its distress has been suffered in front of millions via television and U.N. inquiries and debates. This is a very different age, and the Africans have not the luxury of discrete rethinking of their original answers to many of these questions.

NOTES

1. At the risk of personalizing this too much, I want to suggest what "rural" can mean. We lived for a year in Zomba, Malawi, the seat of the University of Malawi, home to the Malawian Parliament and colonial capital of Nyasaland. It is situated on a major highway. All of that should produce a fairly dynamic economy, one would think. On the contrary. Among commodities for which we searched in vain at various times: salt and pepper shakers, cottage cheese, coat hangers, whole wheat bread or flour, eggs, mustard, sugar, and table knives. We were told that we did not want to know about the deficiencies of the "general" hospital that served the town. Had we lived in a "real" village far off the beaten track, the list of unavailables would have included virtually everything that an American or Western European takes for granted.

2. The greatest contrast I have witnessed in Africa was in the neighborhood of the Johannesburg stock exchange. Across the street from the 25-story office building was the shop of an herbalist. High-heel-clad women and suited men walked out of the stock exchange building to survey dried baboons and frogs, bins of herbs, bones, roots, and other items which defied description.

3. I am reminded of our night watchman, a necessary presence in poor countries where one's material accumulation must be protected from the masses who have virtually nothing. Perhaps 60 years old, he would bicycle 22 kilometers to work arriving at 6 P.M. and departing at 6 A.M. seven days a week. He had a "farm" on which he sharecropped tobacco for the landowner who was also head of a university department. He had no access to paper with which to make cigarettes, so he regularly solicited old newspapers from us for that purpose. What a cultural gap he crossed every day!

4. I think of an African friend whom we invited for dinner. Preparing the food, the kitchen helper asked what tribe our guest was from. We demurred. When we reported this query to him, he told us that he would never employ someone from another tribe to prepare his food for fear of poisoning.

5. A conversation with our cook in Malawi illustrated this precisely. He paid one-third of his income for private school tuition for his three eldest sons. When I expressed surprise, he explained that he wanted at least one to get into the university so that he would then obtain a "good job" and be able to provide for him in his old age.

6. Meeting with a multiparty group of women, my wife asked that they identify themselves and their parties. A woman from the recently-deposed postindependence party concluded her introduction with, "I love my party."

7. Discussing an impending meeting with chiefs, we asked a local friend about his relationship to his chief. The chief knows everyone in the village, we were told, and can adjudge low-level disputes, but not criminal cases. If someone is digging the potatoes of a neighbor, the chief can render a decision and impose an appropriate fine—e.g., pay the offended party a chicken. This kind of process does not transfer well to a very large society or a very serious matter.

8. Discussing our growing sense of insecurity in Malawi, a U.S. official reported that a quantity of vehicles had just been delivered to the local police. However, they were being used not for law enforcement, but to transfer police to and from work and take them on personal errands.

9. The leader of the Central African Republic, Jean-Bédel Bokassa, renamed it Central African Empire, and had himself crowned in the manner of Napoleon—at inestimable cost. Not surprisingly, his "reign" was neither long nor widely appreciated.

10. I recall talking with a law school professor who was a graduate of the very African institution where he taught and who had received a Ph.D. from a world-renowned British university. He had taken up a position on the faculty only three months earlier, and his comment was, "I will see if this institution is 'stayable.'" Within a few months, he was gone, employed by an IGO.

11. Unfortunately, the AIDS epidemic is accomplishing just this goal in some places. For some hard-hit countries, life expectancy has dropped five to ten years over the past decade; population growth rates are approaching zero in some places.

12. See Fredland, 4ff. for a discussion of this question.

CHAPTER 9

South Africa: A Special Case

I see only one hope for our country and that
is when white men and black men, desiring
neither power nor money, but desiring only
the good of their country, come together to
work for it.

—Alan Paton, in *Cry, the Beloved Country*

South Africans lined up outside a polling station in Soweto, a
black township outside Johannesburg, to cast their first votes in
the election of April1994.

I was moved beyond words by the spirit of for-
giveness and reconciliation that seems to embrace
this new land.

—Hillary Clinton at University of
Cape Town, 1997

Just perhaps Alan Paton's 1960s observation may prove gen-
uinely prophetic. Certainly the behavior of President Nelson
Mandela reflected in both word and deed the requisite attitude
for engendering hope. Fortunately, he was joined by many others
in positions of influence, most notably former President F. W.
DeKlerk, Archbishop Desmond Tutu, and ANC President Oliver
Tambo. As a consequence of the remarkable transformation
which occurred in South Africa in the early 1990s, a most hopeful beacon brightens the future that Africa may conceivably
achieve. Thus, no examination of Africa would be adequate without special attention to South Africa. There is, however, a certain
risk in being too specific, because the peaceful revolution that is
underway will not reach fruition for some time—if ever—if eco-

---

DESMOND TUTU

Desmond Tutu, an Anglican clergyman, attained the position of
Archbishop of South Africa. As a ceaseless worker for peaceful
transition in South Africa, he was recognized around the world
and received the Nobel Prize for Peace in 1993. Upon the acces-
sion of Mandela to power, he was appointed chairman of the
Truth and Reconciliation Commission, a novel institution
designed to elicit the truth about government atrocities in
defense of the old regime in exchange for "reconciliation"—i.e.,
no prosecution.

BIOBOX 9.1

F. W. DEKLERK

F. W. DeKlerk was elected President of South Africa in 1989. Recognizing that the *apartheid* regime was untenable, he commenced a dialogue with Mandela, though he did not release the black leader from jail. Trading majority rule for peace—an end to the increasingly violent campaign of the African National Congress—DeKlerk arranged for the release of Mandela and a referendum on *apartheid*, which was soundly defeated. DeKlerk accepted the vice-presidency under Mandela as a sign of reconciliation, though his political role declined.

He shared the Nobel Prize for Peace with Mandela in 1993.

BIOBOX 9.2

nomic redistribution is a feature of the revolution. Nonetheless, certain realities prevail, and if one is to "understand Africa," attention must be paid to South Africa. The following table presents the political/demographic realities of that country:

As the numbers unambiguously indicate (see table 9.1), the population is virtually three-quarters "African." (Of course, most of the rest of the population is "African" as well if birthplace is the determinant.) As a matter of fact, some whites could be deemed "more African" than some blacks in that they can trace their forebears further back in that same locale. While this argument contains much sophistry, it does highlight the fact that the South African "problem" could never be solved by sending the minority populations back to where they came from.

The first Europeans in South Africa were the Dutch who settled throughout the southeastern half of the country in the seventeenth century, meeting migrating Zulus and others arriving from the North. James Michener vividly captures the emotion of the times in *Covenant*, his lengthy fictionalized history of several

TABLE 9.1

Demographics of South Africa

Population, in "old" pecking order	Total: 38.4 million
White	5.2 million (15%)
Afrikaaner	3.2 million (62%)
English	<2 million (38%—of which 10% Jewish)
Coloured	3.2 million (9%)
Asian	900,000 (2.4%)
Hindu	630,000 (70%)
Moslem	180,000 (20%)
Black	29 million (73%)
Zulu	7.8 million (27%)
Xhosa	7.5 million (26%)
Tswana	3.2 million (11%)
Others	20.5 million (36%)

Source: Data from various sources, ca. 1990.

families. By the twentieth century, the British had replaced the Dutch as the dominant power, though a fiercely nationalistic Boer[1] minority constituted the permanent white underclass.

In 1931 Britain released South Africa into the hands of the white "ruling class." Over time, the multipartite enmities between blacks and whites; Boers and English; Zulu, Xhosa, and other indigenous ethnic groups; and Coloured and Asian required a political solution, which was implemented in the post-World War II era under the leadership of the Nationalist Party. It was termed *apartheid* ("apartness" in *Afrikaans*), which meant supersaturated racial separation of a type this writer never witnessed as a child growing up in segregated South Carolina.

Segregation of schools or hospitals follows fairly logically from the basic premise, but *apartheid* took separation to new levels: Blacks were not permitted to own property outside their designated "tribal homelands" (the policy was termed "influx control") which consisted of 13 percent of the poorest land in the country (for 73 percent of the population). Never could a black supervise the work of a white. Segregation of ambulances caused the deaths of blacks who could not be transported in an ambulance of the "wrong" color, and on and on. The mechanism of control was a passbook verifying the employment of blacks which had to be regularly marked by police. Being on the street without a passbook meant jail, and South Africa had the highest percentage of its population jailed of any country. At no time in modern history has a minority population so dominated a majority as in South Africa between 1950 and 1990.

The *apartheid* regime was, in truth, very cleverly organized from the white perspective. Blacks were essentially erased from their consciousness except for providing menial labor. A black servant might live in quarters behind a comfortable white home, but her/his family was not permitted to be there. "Home" for the servant was a "township"—a black suburb such as the notorious Soweto[2]—where "temporary residence" was permitted. "Home" in the sense of having access to land, etc., was limited to the "homelands," the tribal territories scattered in bits around the eastern part of the country. Black workers who had to commute to their jobs could easily spend two hours a day on the train (if they survived, since violence was a regular feature of train travel in the late stages of the old regime). Highways, even maps, bypassed black areas, so that one could travel the country and be only marginally aware of the majority population.[3]

In an effort to put a better face on the situation, the government termed the policy "separate development" and did all it could to emphasize the cultural gap between races. The implication was that the "homelands" would be developed, and four of ten were actually "given independence" by South Africa, though none was ever recognized internationally.

The life of ANC and subsequently South African President Nelson Mandela essentially chronicles this period of increasing repression followed by a sudden and revolutionary relaxation.

Mandela was imprisoned for various illegalities, including treason for his role in the African National Congress's advocacy of violent attacks, particularly on infrastructure elements. Under growing pressure from internal disobedience, international sanctions, and increasing cleavage within white society, in 1992 President F. W. DeKlerk released Mandela from prison after 27 years and collaborated with him in developing a transitional government which gave way to majority constitutional rule by 1994. In 1999 a second election was held in which Thambo Mbeki, a longtime associate of Mandela, was elected president. This has demonstrated that the cooperation holds, and all sides have accepted the fate the voters chose.

Not all has been easy, of course. Blacks on both the left and the right have not been supportive. The multiracial Communist Party, a supporter of the ANC, has been less than enthusiastic about collaboration with the former government, as has the Pan-Africanist Congress. On the right, Chief Mangosutu Buthelezi, supported variously by the white government and the Central Intelligence Agency, held out for a more conspicuous role in the transition. And predictably, the unreconstructed segregationists on the white right lobbied for a separate white province. Nonetheless, a transitional government was elected in 1994 with Mandela as President, and two vice-presidents, one from the ANC and the other former President DeKlerk, a truly remarkable outcome.

If ever a state had promise, South Africa does. Its GNP is half that of all sub-Saharan Africa, but that wealth is very maldistributed: 1980 per-capita income was US$9,136 for whites, $3,836 for Asians, $2,857 for Coloureds, and $2,056 for blacks. Still, this puts South Africa's blacks far ahead of most of their brethren in the rest of Africa—a point that was regularly made by the whites and their supporters.

On the mineral front, South Africa is one of the world's best-endowed states, roughly comparable to Australia, Canada, or Russia in percentages of the world's minerals in its reserves—e.g., chromium, 84 percent; gold, 50 percent; manganese, 78 percent; platinum, 74 percent; and vanadium, 47 percent. Additionally, it produces the major portion of the world's gem diamonds; indeed, DeBeers, a South African firm, has traditionally controlled the international diamond market.

As the premier economy in Africa, South Africa boasted in 1985 of a trade surplus of US$5.87 billion. Its primary trading partners in 1985 were the world's major industrial trading states—the United States, Japan, the United Kingdom, and Germany. All in all, one might expect that South Africa has great potential. It does, but it faces the daunting task of creating equity—responding to escalated expectations—among its entire population, not just assuring the comfortable lifestyle of its white minority.

Despite its many advantages, 25 percent of South Africa's population has neither home, nor job, nor land. When, as one white South African commented, virtually "everyone" has a swimming pool, the pressure for a representative government to institute change can rise to proportions that make orderly devolution of political and economic power untenable. That is the conundrum that South Africa faces. It begins with substantial pluses: great natural wealth, a middle class, educated workers and civil servants, enthusiastic foreign investment, ample trading opportunities, and first-class infrastructure. On the negative side, it faces uncertainty about what will follow Mandela with the charismatic leader no longer president, an ongoing flight of resources and trained white citizens, pervasive poverty and instability, and persistent tensions within the black community and between racial groups. For the first few years of its new existence, South Africa developed impressively well; it can only be hoped that development will continue.

South Africa is *sui generis*; other African states cannot learn much from studying its progress, except in the most general way. The unique combination of natural wealth, trained workers, incredible physical beauty, and a higher level of development than any other African state sets it apart from the norm. Regional arrangements—e.g., Preferential Trading Area, COMESA, or SADC, which are currently jockeying for dominance in a very crowded market—could provide an opportunity for South Africa to be an "engine of growth" for the region, if conditions evolve to make that possible. South Africa has some potential for improving the lives of Angolans or Malawians, but it cannot stretch its resources to reach Sierra Leone or Somalia, however desirable that may be. The greater likelihood, however, is that South Africa's generosity will be curtailed and competitive relationships will evolve, especially when the country is surrounded by so much need on top of its own politically pressing needs. There are two hopeful signs: Foreign investment has grown geometrically and the current political leadership, including the former white president DeKlerk, has demonstrated great restraint and statesmanship. One can only hope. . . .

NOTES

1. The language of the Dutch population in South Africa is *Afrikaans*, a corruption of Dutch. *Boer* is Afrikaans for "farmer," which properly described the original settlers.

2. Soweto, an abbreviation of Southwest Township, was the location of the agglomeration of perhaps a million black citizens. Blacks were permitted to temporarily "sojourn" in such townships, but they did not exercise the usual privileges of citizens. Often families were separated, the women, children, and elderly remaining in the "homelands" attempting to till the unforgiving soil. Some townships were so remote that two-hour commutes were not unheard of, consuming a significant portion of workers' earnings. Paradoxically, a middle class did emerge in the black communities—small merchants, professionals—and middle-class neighborhoods grew up amidst the seas of slums.

3. To demonstrate that all was not simple, however, the writer recalls that just opposite the entrance to the black township of Soweto was a BMW dealership! It was said, interestingly, that South Africa had the highest rate of BMW ownership in the world (since the cars were often a fringe benefit for white managers).

CHAPTER 10

Africa and the International System

Whatever happens we have got
The Maxim gun and they have not.

—Hilaire Belloc

Hundreds of thousands of Kenyans live in this Nairobi slum, lacking all the necessities of modern living. Robbery, prostitution, and murder are part of everyday life. The struggle for survival inevitably drives out all thought of such larger issues as democracy and investment.

The international system into which African states were welcomed in the 1960s and after was in the process of moving to a new distribution of influence dominated by two hostile superpowers, a changing group of middle-range powers, and a rapidly growing collection of minor states, including much of Africa. The oldest active participants in the system (excluding China which had been largely isolated from the European-Middle East axis) were in Europe. While they were adjusting to a new situation in which their power, wealth, and influence (read *colonies*) were waning, they still dominated the political culture of the international system. And it was into this culture that the new African states were ostensibly welcomed.

The strategic view that had emerged earlier in modern Europe reckoned that Europe occupied the political core of the globe. On its periphery lay the southern Mediterranean coast, the Middle East, and Russia. Beyond that lay unimportant regions such as Asia, Africa, and the Americas. A corollary to this view held that control of the core (Europe) would assure control of the periphery which, in turn, would assure control of the outlying regions. It was this kind of thinking that led to the rush for colonies in Africa, and that persisted as European states sought the best of both worlds—magnanimously granting independence to colonies but remaining involved in their basic activities such as banking, commerce, defense, and diplomacy. The relationship was much more than informal penetration.

The most fundamental characteristic of the international system is anarchy. There is no overarching authority and no international consensus that one is needed. Nonetheless, with the founding of the United Nations an international consensus on values began to develop (for instance, the values enshrined in the Universal Declaration of Human Rights). However, superpower strategic considerations always took precedence over philosophical principles, and the Africans were regularly rebuffed when they couched their arguments in philosophic terms.

AFRICA AND THE COLD WAR

In the early post-World War II years, general international conflict was assiduously avoided by the major powers, primarily because the onset of the nuclear age promised horrific devastation in large-scale war, but also because of the redeployment of influence from Western Europe to the United States and the Soviet Union. Most important for Africa were the involuntary roles thrust upon many states as proxies in Cold War conflicts between the superpowers. Since neither the Soviet Union nor the United States was interested in provoking the other to direct conflict, their maneuvering was carried on through surrogates. One example was the installation of President Mobutu in Zaire by the CIA and the implicit and explicit U.S. support of his repressive regime. The British, French, and Belgians were unrepentant neocolonialists seeking to preserve their influence in former colonies primarily through economic controls.

Africa became involved in the Cold War largely because of preexisting colonial ties, the large proportion of U.N. votes to be found on the African continent (see table 10.1), and concern for strategic interests (e.g., South Africa's geopolitical location and the mineral wealth in several southern locations). So, whether

TABLE 10.1
African Proportion of U.N. Membership

Year	Total Members	African Members	African Percentage
1945	53	2	4%
1952	60	3	5%
1959	83	9	11%
1960	99	24	24%
1965	118	35	30%
1976	147	48	33%
1997	183	53	29%

Source: *United Nations Yearbook.*

interested or not, many African states were drawn into international politics far beyond their ability to sustain participation without relying on external resources. As in a poker game, one had to "ante up" in order to play.

With the proliferation of African states and their concomitant votes in international bodies came a decline in the seriousness which many observers attached to these votes. For example, it was possible to achieve a majority in the U.N. General Assembly with the votes of states that represented no more than 5 percent of the world's GNP or population. The principle of "one state, one vote" (an analogue to "one man, one vote") was embraced without question, depreciating the impact of the decisions of many organizations.[1] Other organizations arose to enable the great powers to manage their essential interests, e.g., NATO, OECD, G–7.[2]

African states, of course, welcomed the new-found role of international player, and they readily adopted certain issues—redistribution of global wealth (the *New International Economic Order* as adopted by the General Assembly in 1973), majority rule

---

THE NEW INTERNATIONAL ECONOMIC ORDER

This U.N. resolution adopted in 1973 mandated a redistribution of the world's wealth from the rich to the poor through a series of specific devices—e.g., lifting of copyright and patent protection to let poor states benefit from the research and inventiveness of the rich. Few of the provisions were ever taken seriously, but they put the poor states on record regarding the world's distribution of wealth and provided those in rich countries with a legitimized framework for arguing the case for redistribution.

BOX 10.1

TABLE 10.2
United Nations Speeches by Africans, 15th–21st General Assembly Sessions*

Topic	15th	16th	17th	18th	19th	20th	21st	TOTAL
Decolonization	370	670	530	430	140	490	630	3,260
South Africa	110	150	160	180	60	170	180	1,110
Economic Aid	220	180	400	350	110	440	490	2,190
Congo	100	50	20	50	30	10	10	270
Human Rights	40	100	140	180	10	320	350	1,140
African Representation	60	60	0	140	30	50	50	440
Disarmament	40	90	100	130	90	190	130	770
Refugees	30	60	70	50	10	80	70	370
China	10	20	30	30	30	50	50	220
International Law	10	20	30	60	10	100	90	320

From: David A. Kay, "The Impact of African States on the United Nations," paper presented at American Political Science Association, November, 1968, p. 25.

*Numbers rounded to nearest 10.

in South Africa (and Namibia), and a few others (see table 10.2). As *causes célèbres* captured the attention of the superpowers with their development assistance programs (and consequently, took priority on the international political agenda), it became profitable for various states to take positions not on the basis of national interest but in response to global political positioning. Unfortunately, since so little power underlay African political rhetoric, the only way Africans could be effective was by taking relatively extreme stands—e.g., anti-Israel, pro-wealth redistribution, and pro-arms control.

What were the international political objectives of the "typical" African state following independence? Assuming rational decision making, it is axiomatic that a system seeks, first of all, its own survival; it follows that all African states sought internal stability and external security. These were not easily achieved by the relatively impotent African systems. The older states in the system had the advantage of fully settled borders and national identities, but African states lacked both these rather modest assets.

The internal cohesion which had resulted from anticolonial politics soon vanished in most places as local politics displaced anticolonial activities. If a charismatic leader was present—Nkrumah in Ghana, Nyerere in Tanganyika, Kaunda in Zambia, Senghor in Senegal—it was possible for a government to generate legitimacy and solidarity. However, more often competing loyalties in the form of ethnic, religious, and regional identities erupted into conflict when the larger external enemy disappeared. External threats in the form of cross-border attacks were practically nonexistent; most states were so preoccupied with establishing internal legiti-

---

ORGANIZATION OF AFRICAN UNITY

Books and articles abound, but a brief sketch of Africa's "United Nations" can offer a better understanding of what is going on there. Founded in 1963, this organization has articulated the African perspective on many topics over the years, particularly on South Africa, nonalignment, and the New International Economic Order. The individuality expressed by newly independent African states coupled with their penurious condition hampered the effectiveness of the OAU, and it has been essentially tangential to most of Africa's significant developments over thirty years.

It has established cooperation with most U.N. technical agencies to share data on a continent-wide basis. That has been useful but relatively insignificant.

BOX 10.2

---

macy that they did not reach beyond their own borders. It was, incidentally, an article of faith in the **Organization of African Unity** from its founding in 1963 that colonially-prescribed boundaries would be respected because no alternative arrangements would elicit the requisite support to render them practical.

Early on, the domestic politics of every state took on the theme of "development," whatever that meant. Always, it was within the context of a poor Africa vis-à-vis a wealthy world, and promises were made internally about the better future to come while blandishments were delivered abroad to garner assistance in achieving that future. Unfortunately, these efforts were confounded by the anticolonial policies advocated by many states. These policies confronted the remaining colonial tentacles entwined in the local economies—banking and finance, tourism, and manufacturing/importing/exporting. In time, the inherent corruption of this dichotomy led to political neuroses, and leaders eagerly collaborated with colonial interests behind the scenes while ranting against them in public pronouncements.[3]

Building on the dominance of democratic socialism in much of Western Europe and on the ideology of African socialism, most African states proclaimed themselves noncapitalist (if not anticapitalist). At the same time, the international economy was increasingly dominated by the United States, and newly-emerging capitalist regimes rose out of the reversal of the dominant African paradigm in the 1980s, largely as a consequence of structural adjustment programs imposed by international financial institutions accompanied by the collapse of communism.

The absence of agreed-upon principles reflected the anarchy of the system with the consequence that no state caught in the wheels of great power machinations could expect assistance. Francophone Africa relied upon France for military support in the event of internal crises; similarly, the three former British colonies in East Africa summoned British assistance to squelch military coups in their early years. Such help was always ad hoc and unpredictable, and it never came from the international community acting as a whole.

POSTINDEPENDENCE OBJECTIVES

The objectives that Africa sought internationally were not surprising, and they were joined by other Third World states from Asia and Latin America. First, there was stability. Even though they had achieved sovereignty by disturbing the international order, as putative participants they did not want to "tinker" with the resulting structure, which explains why none of the ill-suited boundaries of African states has been readjusted.

INSIGHT: A PERSONAL INSIGHT INTO POVERTY

The overarching reality about Africa is that its people are poor. In the past decade they have grown relatively poorer, their infrastructure has decayed, and instant communications has made more and more Africans increasingly aware of their relative deprivation. It is not possible to think about Africa without being oppressively cognizant of this fact. I walk the road in front my house and normally see many times as many people walking as driving; several times more men and boys bicycling than driving; women and girls, and occasionally boys or men, carrying huge loads of firewood for cooking. About half the people I see are barefoot, and some of the remainder are shod only in "flip-flops." People pedal themselves in wheelchairs, like the chap who periodically wheels himself to our door to sell a half dozen lemons or two pieces of cassava root. Malawi—slightly poorer than average—is preeminently poor. Whatever secondary characteristics one may observe, poverty is the overriding reality. Approximately 200,000 people in this country of over 10 million have regular incomes. The gardener we employ is well-paid at about US$36 per month (plus two meals a day and some clothes) for a 70-hour week. Such conditions prevail only because if our gardener balked, a line of replacements would form at the first hint of a vacancy.

Second, they sought autonomy and noninterference in their affairs. They regularly adopted anticolonial and anti-Western stances. Their political rhetoric played well with the Soviet Union but was widely dismissed in the West as typical of immature systems. There was a certain juvenile pride in the manner in which newly-established states went about displaying their independence. They were like burgeoning adults who flex their social muscles to test the limits of societal control.

In one way, Africans can be proud that they have protect-

This widespread poverty and the typically wealthy elite combine to create a need for what must be the largest category of formal employment in Africa—security guards. Our "standard" Western-style house with three bedrooms, two baths, etc., proclaims itself to all who see it is as a center of relative wealth; inside are clothes, food, towels, not to mention a camera or computer. It cannot be left unattended for even a brief time for fear of thievery, so we employ a gardener, a cook-housekeeper, and a night watchman—all to protect our island of materialism in a vast sea of need. Security businesses prosper, and the daily parade of night guards trekking to their appointed posts is remarkable. Still, the ranks of the unemployed are overflowing. Because of the chronic unemployment, there are large movements of migrant labor around Africa, especially to South Africa to work in the mines.

This individualistic perspective is a metaphor for the larger global economy. Though the metaphorical international need for the night watchman is less clear, since the rich are protected from the poor by oceans, the relative gap is there. An African family of a dozen or twenty may live in a one-room dwelling with a few pieces of cooking equipment and a radio, if its members are fortunate.

Zomba, Malawi, 1997

ed their economies from direct outside manipulation, as indicated by the low levels of direct foreign investment (column 1, appendix B). On the other hand, the reluctance of foreign investors to participate in most of the African economy demonstrates lack of investor confidence in the continent's future. Except in states like Gabon (where there is oil), there is relatively little trade in terms of GDP. African production is low-value in terms of earning foreign income, and poor Africans can demand few imported goods. These factors combine to keep trade at a low level.

Economic development was high on the new states' agenda, of course. Many U.N. agencies—e.g., UNICEF, UNDP, UNHCR, IMF, World Bank, UNESCO, WHO, FAO—were, in effect, redistributive mechanisms which extracted some wealth from rich states and redistributed it to the poor. Since private investment was seen as unacceptably risky in most African states, the most popular mechanisms for introducing new technology and skills had to be bilateral—i.e., government-to-government—or multilateral through international organizations. This continued apace and still characterizes most resource transfers to Africa.

Confronting a Western cultural milieu that was fairly homogeneous, particularly in its international political stances, the Africans found themselves without a unifying concept. *Négritude*, African socialism, and Pan-Africanism[4] all emerged to fill this need, but none of them proved adequate to the immense challenges of the task. They provided no sufficiently compelling *zeitgeist* to counter the rush toward Western values and material possessions. Abdul Said put it this way: "[They sought] further freedom through nationalism, progress through a special kind of socialism . . . order, dignity, and self-expression through federalism or Pan-Africanism, [and] . . . security through neutralism" (p. 66).

The "bottom line" for any state is survival. The less powerful a given state, the more its policies will focus on this basic concern. Since no African state was remotely powerful, survival was regularly in question. They might employ noisome rhetoric, but they did not usually concern themselves with following up on it.

The typical African political system was very different from the prior dominant paradigm of Western European democratic socialism. There was genuine equality among them, if for no other reason than that all African states were equally impotent. They could pronounce, but they could not produce. Their vaunted **nonalignment** was compromised in the interest of resource acquisition as they courted, and were courted by, the Soviet Union, the United States, and occasionally lesser powers— Britain, France, Japan, Germany.

African states learned early on that small states are different from large states. Before Africa's entry onto the world stage, there was no typology of small states. Places like Iceland, Monaco, and Haiti were, in effect, dependencies of larger states or so peripheral that their existence really did not matter in the international political system. Now an international system existed a third of whose members were not only very small powers, but untraditionally vociferous ones as well. As they were learning

---

NONALIGNMENT

This term from the early days of the Cold War describes the posture of those states that wished to avoid entanglements in the superpower conflict in the belief that it would be the most beneficial stance they could adopt. Led by India, Algeria, Egypt, Tanzania, Yugoslavia, and others, the non-aligned movement grew to include about half the states of the world, as reflected in U.N. votes.

The payoff generally came when a nonaligned state played off one superpower (or its surrogate) against the other. For example, the leader of the nonaligned state would reason, *If superpower A does not give me X, then superpower B will. Thus we will be indebted to B.* Superpower A, so threatened, would then grant the nonaligned state's request.

BOX 10.3

---

proper conduct in their new arena in a new age, the "solid citizens" of that arena had to learn to respond to their rambunctiousness without taking offense.

In addition to active memberships, particularly in the U.N. system, there was shortly established the Organization of African Unity along with many other regional manifestations of international collaboration and cooperation. Some African states belonged to as many as 75 international organizations (see table 10.3). Some tried to remain nonaligned, but that was obviated by the requirements of the Cold War.

Cumulatively, many countries lack the resources available in a major city in the West. But needs and aspirations accumulate: to repair roads inherited from colonial times; to construct sec-

TABLE 10.3
African Memberships in International Organizations, 1990

	N =	Avg. No. Memberships	Range
All Africa	52	53.4	2–111
Minus Namibia, So. Africa	50	55.3	14–111
"New" States (post-1968)	11	22.8	16–48
"Old" States (pre-1968)	41	60.8	10–111
East Africa	3	74.3	72–77
British Colonies	14	45.4	16–74
French Colonies	19	73	18–111
Portuguese Colonies	5	18.2	14–22
Maghreb	5	40.5	40–41
Microstates	7	18.7	14–24

Data from Richard Fredland, *A Guide to African International Organizations*, London: Hans Zell Publishers, 1990, p. 267.

ondary schools so girls can attend in the same numbers as boys; to build hospitals to treat an outbreak of disease X, Y, or Z; to maintain an embassy in yet another capital city; and on and on.

And to pay for this? There are taxes which are paid only by the few law-abiding, relatively well-off citizens. They, however, have an incentive to conceal their incomes by operating in the informal sector or opening the proverbial "Swiss bank account." What about selling what exists in surplus? If it is a mineral product—cobalt, copper, bauxite—there are no facilities for processing the ore nor is there a local market in which to sell it. Instead it is shipped out in bulk to have its value enhanced in the mills of industrialized states. Thus, the aluminum widget that costs $20 in a Western store (or $35 in an African store) may contain bauxite ore that brought Ghana (or Trinidad) no more than a few cents.[5] If income is derived from agriculture, the problems are manifold. Price is determined by supply in the international marketplace. If Brazil decides to expand its coffee or banana production and if shipping costs are equal to or less than those from Africa, the banana market may shift to Brazil with no thought to the consequences for African farmers.

REGIONALISM

One mechanism available to African states to bolster their bargaining position, at least in theory, is a regional approach to the global economy. The model of the European Union which has coincided with several economic and political revolutions in Europe, has been imitated repeatedly—but halfheartedly—in Africa. Another appealing model is OPEC, a resource cartel.

On neither count has Africa been successful, however. There are prerequisites for successful regional organizations or cartels, but Africa possesses few of them. For **regionalism** to succeed, several of the following conditions must be present: complementarity of economies, political will, apparent benefits greater than apparent costs, and functioning markets. Two "regional" arrangements incorporating a number of African states are the British Commonwealth and the French *Communauté*. These are groups of former colonies (including Canada, Australia, Botswana, and Sierra Leone in the former; Gabon and Guyana in the latter). The "benefit" that accrued to African states was the opportunity to sell primary products in the European market unfettered in return for giving the former metropole unfettered access to the African markets for its manufactured products. So Zambia sells copper to England and purchases heavy machinery

---

REGIONALISM

This has become a popular economic reaction to a global economy. No state—not even the largest—is autarchic, completely self-sufficient. Cooperating with neighbors to obtain resources and access to markets benefits all sides in the aggregate even though it imposes occasional costs in the short run. Africa has been slow to make serious attempts at regionalism because of (a) the newness of most of its states and (b) the lack of potential intraregional trade. Most African imports are manufactured goods, and most exports are mineral and agricultural products. That leaves little to be traded among the states, which diminishes the potential benefit of regionalism.

The participation of South Africa with its well-developed manufacturing and transportation sectors, may engender cooperation, however. **Example:** The East African Community of the 1960s and 1970s was a good example; but there is no current example of the same quality, though SADC (Southern African Development Community) may in time achieve comparable significance.

BOX 10.4

(perhaps with copper components)—and this exchange is subject to the "terms of trade" discussed below. The former colonies are trapped at every level, and the flexibility always appears to lie with the rich states.

A cartel, on the other hand, needs none of the similarities required for regional economic groups. The success of the cartel hinges on the product:

1. Do the cartel members have something close to a corner on the market?
2. Is the product (such as oil) in great demand and technologically irreplaceable? (During OPEC's initial muscle-flexing, automobile drivers in the West demonstrated that they would tolerate a five- or six-fold increase in gasoline prices and still buy at roughly the same rate. There is no consumer-acceptable substitute for the gasoline engine to date.)
3. Is the product storable—i.e., if we cannot get our announced price today, can we hold on to the product indefinitely till consumers beg for it? (With oil, yes; bananas, no.)

Africa has suffered one more element of economic disadvantage: an unfavorable trend in terms of trade (table 5.2), i.e., the *relative* value of commodities. For example, if I have a bicycle and you have groundnuts (peanuts), a rate of exchange can be established by which the bicycle is exchanged for a certain quantity of groundnuts. Both have value in the general marketplace. Now, if your neighbor can offer kiwis or macadamia nuts, or if I can add gears to the bicycle, the terms of trade will change. Meanwhile, there is not much you can do to groundnuts to raise their relative value—unless you can afford the machinery to manufacture and package peanut butter—but you still need to trade them for a bicycle. My bicycle, however, has become more expensive, and your groundnuts less expensive over time. Thus, the terms of trade have worsened for groundnut growers—through no fault of their own. This, in effect, is what has happened across the board for the relative prices of primary vis-à-vis manufactured goods since African independence. In other words, the African farmer may produce just as much as she did twenty years ago, but it purchases relatively less in the global market place.

Given the cavernous gap in per-capita GDP between Africa and the rich states of Europe and North America as reflected in life expectancy of 75 years versus 50 years, one would expect a persistent and substantial flow of resources toward Africa in an effort to bridge the gap. Despite development assistance to sub-Saharan Africa in excess of $50 billion during the 1980s, the gap has widened.

Financial progress is not the only measure, however. It is useful to note the "human development index" (HDI) developed by the UNDP.[6] The HDI measures education (as indicated by adult literacy, life expectancy at birth, and per-capita purchasing power). Scores range from zero to one. Of the 30 states for which there are data, the HDIs for 60 percent of them are below their GDP rankings—i.e., the population in 60 percent of African states is less well off in terms of human development than are people in other states with similar situations. The point is that Senegal, with a GDP per capita of $1,800, has an HDI similar to those of Sudan and Uganda, which have GDPs of $1,100 and $1,480, respectively. Those governments have achieved greater human development with fewer resources–despite the political instability of the latter two.

One remarkable finding—though it's based on only one year's data—is that of the ten states receiving the most development assistance per capita in 1987, only three (Lesotho, Zambia, and Central African Republic) were among the top ten in HDI rank. Grand conclusions are not possible from such fragmentary data, but they do suggest that states which attract the greatest amount of outside assistance are not necessarily those which achieve the highest levels of human development.

Through a combination of all these circumstances, the "average" African is less well off today than at independence thirty years ago. Unless a broad change of heart rearranges the operation of the international marketplace—and that seems highly unlikely—the Africans' condition will likely continue to deteriorate. (Another complication in this consideration is that the groundnut farmer may have several more children than she had the last time she needed a tractor, so there are more mouths to feed, and minds to be educated and bodies to be clothed. Meanwhile, the worker on the bicycle assembly line in a relatively industrialized country has fewer children, but still has increased material needs.)

Finally, given the state of economic prosperity coupled with the glut in the international financial markets in the 1970s because of the vast sums of "petrodollars" accumulated in oil-exporting states,[7] banks in the West (Europe and North America) had money to lend beyond what their markets demanded. In effect, bankers went shopping for borrowers. Africa with its infinite supply of unmet needs was a ready-made market, so loans were made as much to answer bankers' needs for income as to meet Africa's development requirements.[8] But sooner or later, loans have to be repaid, and unfortunately this came to pass after the terms of trade had worsened. So the loan that could have been repaid out of two years' exports of X now requires perhaps five years' exports, and other economic relationships have also been worsening.

During the Cold War, control of the system was politically in the hands of the superpowers and, to a much lesser extent, of their proxies inside and outside Africa. With the decline of ideology in the international arena came a corresponding rise in the influence of economics. Economics has always been the underlying theme of politics, but it has taken on new legitimacy in the present system. "Self-interest" was a pejorative concept in the post-World War I era of triumphant idealism. Ideology was the predeterminer of all strategic decisions during the Cold War. We have, however, entered the age of the European Union (with its aspirations to a single currency for all of Western and Central Europe), the World Trade Organization (with its promise of declining worldwide trade restrictions), and increasingly open borders (with international trade growing much faster than domestic manufacturing).

The pervasive control exercised by opposing ideological camps during the Cold War extended to localized and even domestic conflicts. The superpowers were preoccupied with avoiding escalation into nuclear war, which meant controlling any local conflicts with the potential to precipitate such escalation. Further, several Cold War confrontations outside Africa—the Cuban Missile Crisis, Vietnam, Afghanistan, various eruptions in the Middle East—attracted superpower attention, further relegating Africa to a "back burner."

The United Nations, which had proved so welcoming at the time of independence, became less and less useful to Africa. Submerged in superpower hostility, the U.N. was paralyzed when it came to major conflict resolution issues. Pronouncements (as opposed to actions), however, were under the influence of the Third World majority—the "Group of 77"—in the General Assembly where the superpower veto did not apply. There, they could regularly muster the votes to delineate policy, e.g., the New International Economic Order demanding a redistribution of the world's wealth. Still, they did not have the political muscle to make anything happen. Two political issues on which Africa regularly pronounced were *apartheid* in South Africa and Nambia and the Israeli-Palestinian conflict. Over time, talk replaced deeds, and the U.N. became polarized into a Third World cabal in one arena and a superpower debating society in the other. As rhetoric replaced action, small states became increasingly strident in order to be heard in the international arena. This in turn increasingly alienated the core Western states, fostering outright hostility in the United States in the 1980s. With the end of the Cold War, however, the United Nations regained some of its potential as the world's first line of response to conflicts threatening regional stability. This portends well for Africa.

The anarchy which dominated the international arena beyond the United Nations relegated Africa to yet another minor role. African states were completely incapable of projecting power beyond their borders even if they managed to fully extend their writ within their own borders. This drove them further and further into the realm of rhetoric as opposed to action, an area reserved for superpowers and near-superpowers—i.e., the West and the Soviet bloc.

So while African states have been present at the transformation of the international political system, their impact has generally declined relative to that of other countries in the world. Africa seems doomed to remain a peripheral actor in the post-Cold War era as economics dominates international relations and ethnic conflict persists. A significant consequence of the dominance of economics is the emergence of African regional efforts at peacekeeping. The first such effort occurred in 1997 with the creation of a force composed of soldiers from eight members of SADC. In West Africa ECOWAS fielded a force consisting primarily of Nigerian troops to respond to chaos in Liberia and Sierra Leone, and that action was subsequently legitimized by the United Nations. Both examples are still in their incipient stages.

There is no future for Africa apart from the international system.[9] Whether one is pessimistic or optimistic regarding Africa's future, that future will be inextricably tied to the economic and political machinations of the global system. Whether or not there is a "new international order," there is an international system, and Africa cannot withdraw from it. Africa exists in a dependent relationship with the major powers, a situation which it cannot reverse and cannot wish away. Perhaps the post-Cold War consensus emerging in the United Nations portends a new standard of international behavior—the U.S. training of an African quick-response force, for example that will be helpful for Africa.[10]

NOTES

1. Africa's dominance of the United Nations was not so complete as these numbers might suggest, however. The major international players were present in all venues while the Africans (unless one accepts Egypt as African) were largely confined to the General Assembly. Further, their impressive percentage did not produce an African Secretary General until 1997.

2. NATO: North Atlantic Treaty Organization; OECD: Organization for Economic Cooperation and Development; G–7: Group of Seven (major financial powers): Canada, France, Germany, Italy, Japan, the United Kingdom, and the United States, with Russia as an observer.

3. Eritrea's independence from Ethiopia was as much a restoration of the status quo as a revision.

4. *Négritude* is a concept developed by black leaders—W.E.B. DuBois, Marcus Garvey, Kwame Nkrumah—early in the twentieth century. It defined the common culture of all Africans, whether in Africa or in the diaspora.

Pan-Africanism was the political concept enunciated primarily by Kwame Nkrumah at the time of Ghana's independence (1956) which advocated a politically unified Africa.

African socialism was the political-economic notion advocated vigorously by Julius Nyerere of Tanzania. It rejected Western capitalism and imperialism in favor of an egalitarian system more beneficial to impoverished Africans.

None of these concepts is significant today.

5. A microcosm of this can be seen in the fishing-fly factory near our home in Malawi. Norwegian fishhooks are merged with feathers shipped from England by African labor to create 10,000 different flies. My calculation is that each hook consumes about three cents worth of local labor—to be sold for many times that price in the West. But as long as someone is willing to tie a fly for the equivalent of three cents, the process continues.

6. United Nations Development Program, *Human Development Report 1998*, pp. 20–21.

7. One of a few African states (Gabon, Libya, Algeria) to benefit from the OPEC price increase was Nigeria, a major oil producer. With the sudden increase in income, grand plans were made to build infrastructure on all fronts. One basic import was cement, and it is said that approximately five hundred ships, several loaded with cement, were waiting to off-load at Lagos, but there was space for only a handful at the docks. The tropical humidity and rain converted the cement before it could be off-loaded, creating substantial cost and no benefit for the Nigerians.

8. The rapid increase in oil prices left many oil-rich states with more income than they could competently spend in the short run. Perhaps upon the advice of Western-trained advisers (no doubt with MBA degrees), these states deposited their gains in solid Western banks, demanding good returns. Since a bank can *pay* interest only if it *collects* interest, the banks were obliged to make

loans with little regard to their quality. Since European practice permits banks to lend several times their capital assets, a petrodollar deposit could, in effect, be loaned out several times over, hopefully assuring the bank that at least *one* of the loans would be repaid; the bank would be in fine shape if all were repaid. But this multiplying of resources without accompanying production created the global inflation that encumbered financial markets in the 1970s. The African contribution to this process was eager acquisition of the "stuff" of modernization from Western markets with borrowed money, with a promise to repay at some indefinite time in the future.

9. The Broadway musical "Stop the World; I Want to Get Off," may offer good music, but its request cannot be taken seriously with regard to international politics.

10. The African Crisis Response Initiative was announced by the United States in 1997 and teams of trainers were dispatched to several African states, including Senegal and Uganda.

Problems and Prospects

The study of international politics has been turned upside down by the ending of the Cold War and all the assumptions about international behavior that accompanied it. The challenge to those of us who focus our attention on the state of things international has been to discern what the next global "situation" will be. "Situation," in this context,

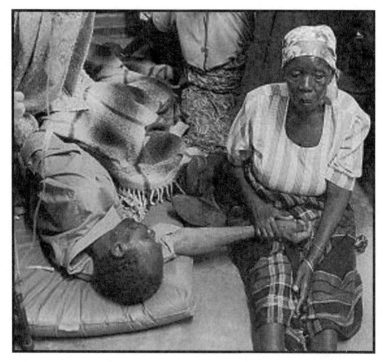

In overcrowded Lilongwe Central Hospital (Malawi), a woman comforts an AIDS-stricken relative. This patient has no bed, only a pad on the floor. Sheets, food, and medication usually have to be provided by the families.

is more accurately explained as "paradigm"—the general framework in which international relations play themselves out.

During the 1990s, opinions about the state of affairs were affected by three broad paradigms: One, posited by Samuel Huntington in 1996, argued that the coming world order will be dominated by what he termed "culture" wars. A second similar, though much more depressing idea, was put forward by Robert Kaplan in *The Atlantic* in 1994. In that dark and alarming piece Kaplan argues that global civilization as it currently exists is unraveling and that the decay has begun in Africa, especially in Liberia and Sierra Leone. A third view, expressed by Ronald Steele among others, is that the world will be dominated by paradoxical forces. Pushing in one direction will be regional arrangements such as the European Union; resisting this momentum will be movements toward fragmentation, such as the break-up of Yugoslavia. Whatever one may think of these arguments, it is instructive to consider their premises, because all are highly pertinent to Africa. Are they predictors of future behavior or null hypotheses?

Huntington argues that the world has replaced the ideological/economic system alignments dominant during the Cold War with cultural (taken broadly) alignments. There are, he maintains, several cultural groupings: Confucian, Western, Middle Eastern, Slavic, Hindu, Latin American, and African. These are combinations of geographic and religio-philosophical aggregates. Where these cultures meet, conflict arises as it has in the former Yugoslavia (a traditional cultural "tectonic" meeting place of Islam from the southeast, Slavic influence from the northeast, and European culture from the northwest). The political subdivisions of the former Yugoslavia and today's emerging polities are very closely aligned with traditional boundaries created by earlier meetings of these cultures. Huntington's prognosis is that we will see large-scale clashes as competing major cultures vie for regional or global resource dominance.

Kaplan, on the other hand, sees nothing but chaos and disaster ahead. When missionary-educated soldiers can execute their former teachers in cold blood as they did in Sierra Leone in the 1980s, he argues, we can never be confident that we have imparted Western values and civilization to anyone. Since civilization at its best is a tenuous balance between forces of order and forces of chaos, Kaplan suggests that very small increments of transformation toward disorder can cause widespread mistrust of systems and can result in general systemic collapse.

Failure, he argues, is on the one hand technological. We simply can no longer sustain life as we in the West have come to know it, much less share that condition with the rest of the world. On the other hand, failure is ideological, as suggested by Abraham Lincoln: "The dogmas of the quiet past are inadequate to the stormy present." Kaplan despairs of developing an effective "central organizing principle" to accommodate the present global pressures from the world's diverse societies. Given the widespread availability of means of destruction, he foresees pervasive murder and mayhem as system after system breaks down.

Steele argues that there are both centrifugal and centripetal forces. The latter are evident in places like the former Czechoslovakia, perhaps in present-day Congo (Zaire), or in the former Soviet Union. At the same time, we see a very tightly integrated European Union, SADC or ECOWAS in Africa, and a strengthened United Nations. It is conceivable that both forces can coexist and that existing states can fragment and then recombine with neighboring fragments in new economic arrangements.

While we cannot—nor should we attempt to—foresee the future, the potential for a very different world in the next several years will have substantial impact on peripheralized Africa. Whatever future eventuates, Africa will be strongly affected by the dominant forces at work in and among the dominant states.

To be sure, there are other, less dire predictions regarding how the global system will reorganize itself. Some see a revived United Nations taking sufficient control of global exchanges to manage conflict and exploitation, and to protect the weak in the face of growing concentrations of wealth and power. Others propose a revised "balance of power" with perennially dynamic power centers akin to the European situation between the World Wars (Kennedy). Still others suggest—or wish earnestly for—global government, a benign administration which manages power and resources for the benefit and security of all.

These women in Bauchi, Nigeria, are attending a literacy class. Obviously, education is proceeding painfully slowly against the immense obstacles that confront any African leader's efforts at modernization.

How is all this relevant to Africa? Can Africa be insulated from these global trends—if they are global trends? Do these scenarios usefully inform African decision makers with regard to policy planning? If Africans accept these arguments, what appropriate steps should they take to prepare themselves for the future? How much should they invest in the belief that one of these directions is the way the world will evolve?

Reports indicate that World Bank economists will soon issue a study showing that the billions of foreign aid "dollars" that have flowed to Africa, *inter alia*, have had little or no impact on economic development.[1] Whatever their economic arguments, there is evidence of "recipient fatigue" in parts of Africa. We have heard about donor fatigue—that condition in which agencies or countries providing assistance become jaded or exhausted from meeting persistent needs and let their interests wander to other pursuits—a logical consequence of the findings of the economists mentioned above. It is equally the case that those who receive eventually weary of being recipients. There is the implicit expectation that those who receive will receive enthusiastically and gratefully time and again. While this may be the case for some period of time or in relation to some exchanges, it is more probable that recipients' gratitude wears thin, just as giving does. But the syndrome of recipient fatigue is a difficult, if not impossible, one to overcome. Gratitude may give way to cynicism or even anger, but the persistence of the need leaves political leaders no choice but to continue to seek assistance.

Recent years have seen increased interest in Africa on the part of the United States. We have made investments in South Africa, become involved in policing several instances of disorder, and in other ways given more attention to the continent than in previous years. The Russians, on the other hand, have withdrawn from Africa almost entirely, and other European powers are continuing in the same postcolonial mode they held to during the Cold War. Japan, the other potential source for development assistance, continues to focus its energies on Asia with some attention to the preeminent potential market of South Africa. Unless a dramatic transformation occurs in relations between the industrial world and the developing states, future relationships will likely be disadvantageous to Africa. Exploitation is characteristic of the exchange of primary goods for manufactured goods—and for some time to come that is likely to be the nature of Africa's economic relationship with the North.

It is simply not conceivable that efficient and effective use will be made, year after year, of the resources transferred from the wealthy West to recipient states in Africa and elsewhere. This leads to cynicism, wastage, a sense of detachment by both parties, and generally ineffective use of resources. At the same time, the process of giving keeps alive the hopes and aspirations of well-intentioned activists (e.g., the new school teacher who receives some books or the agricultural agent who receives new hybrid seeds). The unfortunate outcome of the process is a sense of—and the reality of—dependency that accompanies protracted one-way exchanges. This has soured the entire process and minimizes the effectiveness of the efforts. The resulting suspicion and anomie are harmful to political interactions at all levels.

IMPEDIMENTS TO PROGRESS

There are several major impediments to African progress: One of these, overpopulation, was discussed earlier. Explosive population growth impedes development progress in much of Eastern, Central, and Southern Africa. States with half their populations under the age of fifteen (as is the case in Kenya and Malawi) cannot develop effectively without great resource inputs to provide education and health care for the young. Sadly, the AIDS epidemic may mitigate population growth. With as much as 20–25 percent of a state's population HIV-seropositive, states can anticipate that life expectancy will be dramatically reduced—to around thirty years in some places (see table 11.1).

TABLE 11.1
HIV/AIDS Data for Africa

	1 1990s HIV seropositivy, General Population	2 High Risk	3 Contraceptive used by women various dates	4 Life Expectancy 1996	5 1994–1995
Angola	1.2	—	—	33	46
Benin	1.2	48.9	16.4	54[b]	53#
Botswana	18	60	33	46.5	60
Burkina Faso	6.7	57	7.9	36	46
Burundi	7.6	—	8.7	41.3	43
Cameroon	4.8	16	16.1	39.2	54
CAR	6.9	18.3	14.8	38.5	46
Chad	2.0	13.4	—	34.8	44
Congo	7.2	17.5	21	41.7	49
Cote d'Ivoire	7.7	51.9	11.4	39.2	51
Djibouti	2.4	28.2	—	36	50
Eq Guinea	1.8	5.7	—	36.8	50
Eritrea	—	—	—	39	50
Ethiopia	8.7	43	4.3	35.9	49
Gabon	4.7	16.7	—	40.8	55
Gambia	1.0	13.6	12	32.3	52
Ghana	3.6	72.6	28	45	57
Guinea	1.5	35.6	1.7	33.6	45
Guinea-Bissau	2.6	—	—	34	44
Kenya	11.6	53.5	33	48	55

Country					
Lesotho	4.4	35.6	23	43	60
Liveria	4.0	28.7	6.3	—	49
Madagascar	0.1	.03	17.3	41	56
Malawi	13.6	70.4	13	38	41
Mali	2.5	42.1	6.7	35	48
Mauritania	0.5	0.9	4	38.5	53
Mozambique	2.7	7.6	—	37	45
Namibia	19.8	18.2	28.9	42.5	59
Niger	1.3	23.6	4.4	35	46
Nigeria	2.2	30.5	6	39.5	54
Rwanda	12.2	54.5	21.2	—	41
Senegal	0.3	1.4	7.4	37	53
Sierra Leone	—	26.7	—	31.5	40
South Africa	10	50.3	49.7	49	65
Sudan	4.5	6.6	8.7	—	54
Swaziland	18	35.2	19.8	40	57
Tanzania	6.4	24.4	18.4	40.5	47
Togo	6.8	78.9	33.9	39	53
Uganda	8.8	35.1	14.8	43	40#
Zaire	3.7	29	—	41	50
Zambia	17.1	58	15.2	41.6	43
Zimbabwe	22	86	48.1	45.3	41#

Data in columns 1 and 2 from "Recent HIV Seroprevalence Levels by Country: February 1999," U.S. Bureau of the Census, Health Studies Branch, Research Note No. 26; in column 3 from U.S. Agency for International Development, *World Population Profile*, 1998; in columns 4 and 5 from UNDP, *Human Development Report 1998* and World Bank World Bank Atlas 1998 and U.S. Bureau of the Census, Health Studies Branch, Research Note No. 20, "HIV/AIDS in Africa," December 1995.

a. With the exception of Benin, all states reflect a growth in the use of contraceptives, e.g. Ghana grew from 2% to 28% in 1995, or a stable situation in South Africa: 49.8% in the mid-1970s to 50.3% in 1980.

b. This drop in life expectancy is attributable at least in part to HIV.

AIDS: The Current Catastrophe

Imagine finding one-quarter of the population of your hometown terminally ill. That is the situation in many places in eastern and southern Africa, including the countries of Zimbabwe and Botswana. A substantial portion of patients at clinics for sexually transmitted diseases and virtually all prostitutes in some major urban centers (e.g., Nairobi) are HIV-positive. In extreme instances, entire populations have abandoned some regions because almost the whole "middle" generation has died, leaving orphans to be cared for by grandparents.

Since the 1980s when it was first acknowledged medically, AIDS has taken the lives of some two million Africans and another sixteen million are infected with the HIV virus. The large number of children born to African women and the prevalence of breast feeding have added to the number of children with AIDS.

Poverty in Africa precludes drug use (both the healthy and unhealthy kinds), and there is little acknowledged homosexuality; consequently, AIDS is overwhelmingly transmitted through sex between men and women and perinatally to infants. "Safe" sex remains the only practical remedy for the spread of the disease. The poverty which prevents drug abuse also precludes infant feeding other than by breast, so transmission of the disease to children will persist even after adult behavior changes may affect its spread through sexual intercourse.

Education efforts to reduce the epidemic have encountered many impediments: political denial of the problem, abject poverty that prevents purchase of condoms, fatalism, and periodic false alarms of supposed cures. Admonitions to be monogamous have been interpreted as meaning that one should enjoy the company of one partner at a time. Tradition and religion impose difficulties on education, condom use, and dealing with victims. Poverty precludes seeking treatment, and custom dictates funeral practices that impose increasingly heavy burdens on the economies of several countries.

Those individuals lost to AIDS constitute a major economic loss. They come from the economically most active segments of the population. They are at least somewhat mobile and, therefore, presumably represent greater human capital; and the large numbers of orphans they leave behind portend a generation of poorly educated and inappropriately socialized children. The loss of tourism and investment can only be surmised. A second HIV strain has been found in West Africa, ranging from Angola to Mauritania. It is less prevalent, less deadly, and less easily transmitted.

There is no positive conclusion here. Millions of Africans will die at great cost to their families, businesses, and societies, Until a preventive or affordable cure can be found, the only response is aggressive education. And despair.[2]

Deforestation and Agricultural Degradation

At the rate of as much as 3 percent per annum (see table 11.2), forests are being removed to provide firewood. While this rate is not inherently unsustainable, without aggressive replanting such a situation portends an end to forest land in little over a generation. Forest land is not usually fertile, which compounds the processes that occur. Forests are cleared, which causes erosion and silting of rivers. Farmland is overfarmed, creating a need for relatively expensive fertilizer—which means higher food prices—contributing to further erosion, and giving rise to other indirect consequences. This process is, of course, directly related to population pressures.

Global Economic Gap

The global gap between rich and poor is replicated in many places in Africa, the United States, and elsewhere. So long as there are vast gulfs between the wealthy elite and the impoverished masses, political disorder can be anticipated. No political or economic system can mitigate against hostility engendered by the widening chasm between the rich and the poor.

CHAPTER 11

Post-Cold War Interventions

With the end of the Cold War, foreign intervention by Western powers is likely to subside. The incipient trend of African states taking increasing responsibility for political order (e.g., ECOWAS in Liberia) on the continent can be expected to continue. In more

TABLE 11.2
Environmental Status of African States

State	1 Woodland as Percent of Land Area, 1995	2 Annual Percent Rate of Deforestation, 1990–1995	3 CO2 Emissions per capita (Metric tons), 1995
Angola	17.8	1.0	0.4
Benin	41.8	1.2	—
Botswana	24.6	0.5	1.5
Burkina Faso	15.6	0.7	—
Burundi	12.3	0.4	—
Cameroon	45	0.6	0.3
CAR	48	0.4	0.1
Chad	8.8	0.8	—
Congo	57.2	0.2	0.5
Cote d'Ivoire	17.2	0.6	0.8
Djibouti	—	0	—
Eritrea	—	0	—
Ethiopia	12.3	0.5	0.7
Gabon	69.3	0.5	3.3
Gambia	9.1	0.9	0.2
Ghana	39.7	1.3	0.2
Guinea	25.9	1.1	0.1
Guinea-Bissau	82.1	0.4	0.2
Kenya	2.3	0.3	0.3
Lesotho	0.2	0	—
Madagascar	26	0.8	0.1
Malawi	35.5	1.6	0.1

subtle ways, the wealthy states of the West can be expected to pursue their perceived self-interests with impunity, given the impotence of most African systems. In any case, the general economic climate in which African states must function is well beyond their control.

On the plus side, increased cooperation, particularly with

TABLE 11.2
(continued)

State	1 Woodland as Percent of Land Area, 1995	2 Annual Percent Rate of Deforestation, 1990–1995	3 CO2 Emissions per capita (Metric tons), 1995
Mali	9.5	1.0	—
Mozambique	21.5	0.7	0.1
Namibia	15	0.3	—
Niger	2.0	0	0.1
Nigeria	15.1	0.9	0.8
Senegal	38.3	0.7	0.4
Sierra Leone	18.3	3.0	0.1
South Africa	7.0	0.2	7.4
Sudan	17.5	0.8	0.1
Swaziland	8.5	0	0.5
Tanzania	36.8	1.0	0.1
Togo	22.9	—	0.2
Uganda	30.6	0.9	—
Zaire	48.2	0.7	—
Zambia	42.2	0.8	0.3
Zimbabwe	22.5	-0.6	0.9
For comparison aggregate data for "high human development countries"	21.2	-0.2	12.3

Source: United Nations Development Program, *Human Development Report 1998.*

South Africa, is inevitable. As the producer of about half the wealth in sub-Saharan Africa, South Africa will be a major force regardless of its intentions. Now that its robust economy is under indigenous control, African states are eager to share in its wealth. South Africa will need markets,[3] and neighboring states will need production facilities and job opportunities. Both politically and economically, Africans can be expected to support South Africa so long as it is not perceived as a threat.

Also, despite the failure of regional arrangements up till now, we can expect a greater commitment to regionalization of problems and their solutions. The model of the European Union appeals to Africans, despite their lack of similar preconditions. The "arrangement" between former colonies and the EU establishes a rudimentary infrastructure for some measure of cooperation.

CONCLUSION

Having visited Nairobi, Kenya, more regularly and over a longer period than any other African city, my wife and I have come to feel that we know the place, not well but surely better than as strangers. On the other hand, we have indeed become strangers over time. No doubt our attitudes and perceptions have changed, but Nairobi itself has changed far more. While I hope that my views have become more mature, realistic, and incisive, Nairobi has become meaner, more crowded, less pleasant, and even notorious—precisely because of the forces I propose are integral to understanding Africa.[4]

The economy of Nairobi is, in some quarters, booming. Streets are jammed with automobiles,[5] polluted, and dirty. There are grand highrises, fancy shops, and elegant tourist facilities, but these do not obscure the underlying fact that Kenya's economy is externally controlled, that there is rampant corruption, and that most Kenyans do not share in the benefits of modern society even though they live in the midst of it every day. While new construction proceeds, older buildings molder. New hopefuls arrive or are born while longtime residents await some opportunity that rarely arrives.

People cannot help but see that their society has changed dramatically and continues to change day by day. Nor can they help seeing that, for most of them, the benefits of that change remain unobtainable. They may have to dodge automobiles as they search for scraps of food in the city's wastebins, but they will probably never see the inside of one of those cars. The government announces new schools, wells, clinics, manufacturing facilities, levels of trade, but these advantages somehow rarely get to the people who need them most.

To be sure, the data indicate a growing percentage of adults in Africa who are literate. Infant mortality has declined. More girls are enrolled in elementary and secondary school. More automobiles travel the highways. There is more "stuff." But unhappily, the growth in population has all too often outpaced the "more," and those who were marginalized before remain marginalized today.

An American chaplain on an African campus inadvertently captured the sentiment behind recipient fatigue on a notice he posted outside his office, "Books and Bibles for sale." A wise observer penned the following: "We don't buy; we just receive." An ethos of receiving has developed. Recipients are no longer psychologically prepared to express enthusiasm or to energetically incorporate new assistance into existing situations.

This condition, in conjunction with the rising conservatism of many Western governments, fostered new thinking about assistance and North-South relationships. "Institutional development," "capacity building," "governance," and "civic education" emerged as objectives to replace railroads, dams, buildings, and hospitals. However important infrastructure may be as a development objective, without the capacity to integrate it psychologically and physically into the existing society, there is little point in committing resources to it. This lesson has been learned repeatedly in Africa and elsewhere, but it has taken a long time for institutional responses to develop.[6]

One cannot help but recall the Jahnheinz Jahn quote in the Foreword, "And the one who is addressed, the African, is asked no questions. . . ." He had a valuable insight; and valuable and relevant insights are still available. All too often, new initiatives conclude with, "We will have to ask the Germans . . . the EU . . . the Japanese . . . USAID . . . for funds to build that or install this."[7] This creates an additional difficulty: Assistance is accompanied by well-paid expatriates who hire locals at above-average salaries, equip them with the latest technology, and brook no material discomfort in their personal circumstances. Life is easy; projects are accomplished (or reported to be accomplished— because no one wants to acknowledge failure), and life goes on largely unchanged in the recipient country. As this process of "assisting" matures, detachment grows between the donor and the recipient—another consequence of recipient fatigue.

Cost effectiveness also takes a toll on recipients. Projects involving millions of dollars produce modest effects, and recipients cannot help but wonder how much might have been accomplished had they been consulted on the objectives and design, and been asked to participate in the execution of the exercise. It might be very nice to have a resort hotel on this lake, and it will provide a few menial jobs. But what is really needed is a clinic (or a school or a well or . . .). Local leaders are also part of the problem. It became axiomatic in Malawi that government ministers delivered daily admonitions urging some village or other to engage in "self-help." Meanwhile, the ministers zipped around the country in new luxury autos with extravagant allowances—supported by international donors. Who can take such a process seriously? Only the donor-beneficiaries whose careers are predicated on convincing bureaucrats in Copenhagen, Geneva, Washington, or Paris that they are effectively dispensing worthwhile assistance. Peons observing the process see the hypocrisy clearly. Expatriate observers become more cynical by the day. Local government bureaucrats duplicitously accept all they are offered, assuring the donors that it is going to a good cause—their own.

The National Association of Manufacturers (and other beneficiaries of development largesse in the United States) may object, but the time has come for a complete rethinking of the modus operandi of development assistance, whether it involves human or other forms of capital. No one seriously believes that the primary objective of aid is actually to aid anyone, but the jaded reactions of those who have observed a lifetime of this futile activity is a high price to pay for a relatively small subsidy to the American business community. When welfare in the United States and other Western systems is being rethought, perhaps the focus should be expanded to include the consequences of welfare assistance for both recipients and benefactors. It is not simply a matter of doing more for less; it is a matter of doing something positive for relatively little rather than producing a negative effect at great expense.

As African states move away from centralized planning and toward market economies, the residual need for centralized direction is increasingly apparent. The failure of command economies in Africa is evident, as is the continually expanding gap between the rich and the poor. No sensible observer fails to grasp the weaknesses of command systems—the ennui that traps those with no vested interest in the ownership of means of production; the arbitrary decisions made at "operations central," which may have little or no relevance to reality on the "front line"; the bullheaded persistence in pursuit of a theoretical ideal when reality emphatically shouts, "No!"

The attack on centralization, of course, has been reinforced by the collapse of the Soviet Empire. Many African states spent their first thirty years of independence as client states of one or another superpower, as potential client states, as neoimperial postcolonial remnants, and most often as autocracies or oligarchies. The global revolution which accompanied the collapse of the Soviet Empire sparked efforts by putative democrats in Africa and by various interests outside the continent to press for political and especially economic reforms. In large part this was associated with the immense overhanging debt which many countries accumulated during the 1970s and 1980s. Another contributing factor was the conservative wave which swept through most Western governments during this same period, causing them to employ their leverage as lenders to reverse centralizing tendencies.

Western governments, especially those of the United States and Britain, led the effort in international monetary institutions to press for structural adjustment, accomplishing economically what they had not previously achieved politically. Pressures from this process destabilized already unstable governments and led to political change in some instances, e.g., Zambia. It is not at all clear that such pressured transformation is longlasting,[8] and many African systems remain as unsatisfactory to the West as they were before the process was initiated. The relevance of Western-style democracy to Africa remains to be proven.

In a variety of African societies, we have seen grand colonial institutions such as universities, parks, and homes fall into disrepair, abused by those who inherited them in the independence process. We have seen rampant corruption—as in Zaire where the President extracted money from every level of society, leaving teachers, soldiers, and civil servants unpaid and impoverished while he luxuriated at one or another of his many villas in Africa or Europe. We have seen military coups involving genocide and general mayhem perpetrated by African armies and governments, often armed with weapons supplied by external forces seeking power and influence.

Workers on plantations or in plants owned by investors from the West have been virtually enslaved, their rudimentary skills exploited, their employment rates kept low, and their wages kept paltry to produce relatively cheap products to be sold at substantial profit in the West. Starvation and near-starvation prevail in many countries as they struggle to repay loans to financial institutions headed by executives paid multimillion dollar salaries.

African and expatriate teachers, clergy, and medical personnel labor mightily under unbelievably trying circumstances to bring education, comfort, or improved health to their neighbors. At the same time Africans who have been the beneficiaries of these efforts flee the continent to seek their fortunes in richer, if cooler, climes—the **"brain drain."**[9] A perpetual cycle of educated Africans departing and well-intentioned foreigners arriving cannot provide Africa with direction and stable development.

The Swiss physician-musician Albert Schweitzer established a hospital in rural Congo early in the twentieth century. Its early images were of virtuous service under unbelievably trying circumstances, but upon reflection other images augmented the original ones: When Schweitzer died in 1965, there was not a single individual to whom he had taught his skills, and the hospital was closed. There is no question that his actions were beneficent, but he could have done much more had he imparted education

---

BRAIN DRAIN

This is the attracting-away of African "brains"—educated Africans who prefer to take their chances in wealthier situations rather than return to the poverty and uncertainty of Africa. For example, a physician or professor going to an industralized country should be assured of many times the income he or she could command in a similar African setting. Some random examples specific to different times and places: In Zaire a professor was paid US$20 monthly in the early 1990s. In the late 1990s a counterpart in Malawi might receive US$15,000 plus housing. In the United States, however, either could expect $35–50,000 and access to the latest scholarship and technology—not to mention political freedom and myriad other opportunties.

BOX 11.1

---

along with health care. Africa's needs are so immense that there is much more opportunity for generosity, and an absence of generosity is all the more regrettable when one thinks about the talent that has been lost.

Some years ago, I drafted an essay entitled "800,000,000 Chinese Autos." I hypothesized that if the day ever came when the Chinese owned automobiles at the same per-capita rate as Americans, Detroit might relish the profit from selling some portion of those cars, but the rest of us would have to breathe the pollution, reckon with the increased demand for metals and rubber, cope with the accidents and junk, etc. As Africa seeks to improve materially, it will place growing demands on the earth's resources, which are being depleted or simply transformed technologically into a potentially infinite supply of material goods for all of us. Consider this: Can we afford 650,000,000 Africans imitating our materialistic lifestyle any more than we could handle 800,000,000 Chinese autos? (Collectively, the Chinese are coming closer to that objective than are the Africans.) Africans at least do not have to cope with industrial pollution. In addition, though this argument has been made on the materialistic level, one cannot ignore the spiritual and social aspects of a transformation that is aggressively sought by most countries and political leaders without sufficient thought to consequences, intended and unintended.

The implicit questions to ask regarding Africa's future, regardless of social developments, are these:

- What should Africans reasonably and responsibly want for themselves—politically, economically, communally?
- Even if they can acquire the requisite resources and exercise sufficient control over them, should Africans be content to rush headlong toward the model of the industrial, consumerist West?
- What kind of state system can African polities reasonably sustain?
- How much regional cooperation is useful? Is there the political will to create it?

- How can non-Africans suggest that Africans should engage in self-limiting behavior or seek to halt their development process many stages short of the level the West has enjoyed for many years?
- Have the past thirty years of development effort taught us something that we are overlooking? Could we learn more by taking a different view of the process? Perhaps an African perspective?
- What variables other than those we have considered will lead us to a more optimistic or pessimistic conclusion about what Africa is becoming?

To put an understanding of Africa into a consolidated form is very difficult, first, because it is an extraordinarily complicated place; and second, because of all the caveats necessary to communicate the nuances. Still, some general conclusions are possible:

1. Africa is very poor and will likely remain poor for the near term. If population can be controlled, perhaps conditions will emerge for genuine and appropriate material and social progress. A longer view—one that is politically irrelevant for extant governments on the continent—might be more optimistic, depending upon continuation of incremental economic growth, absence of catastrophes, and sustainment of technological progress to bring new products relevant to Africa to market.

2. The global marketplace has moved into such high gear that economic entities which have conventionally been at the bottom of the global "food chain" find themselves increasingly irrelevant; so Africa may find, now that its turn has finally come to occupy the bottom rung of the global economic ladder, there *is* no bottom rung. Between robotics and global communications, there are fewer and fewer remaining opportunities for simple, low-cost, unskilled human labor in today's international economy.

3. Culturally, Africa has been destroyed (see Box 11.2.) The headlong desire to imitate the materialism of the West has transformed all Africans (and everyone else on the planet) into aspiring, if not actual, consumers. It will be years before Africans on a large scale acquire the resources to

WANANGWA'S CULTURAL PARADOX

Wanangwa was one of the brightest students in my class at the University of Malawi. He could discuss social science with great sophistication, humor, and knowledge. He was very plausibly planning to attend graduate school in political science in Britain.

One day he came to class in a bright white shirt and stylish tie—not an altogether uncommon sight on the campus. I commented on his appearance. Later he came to me and explained that it was the anniversary of his father's death, and he always remembered it by dressing accordingly. On another occasion he told me that no one in his family had been given Christian or English names, hence his Wanangwa, a reflection of his grandfather's insistence on maintaining cultural traditions.

Symbolically his schizophrenic behavior bespeaks the cultural difficulties confronting many, if not most, Africans. On one hand they share a craving for cultural identity and pride—a universal sentiment. Yet on the other hand they desire to become as thoroughly modern as possible, so they dress in a style that is certainly not traditional—and is undeniably Western.

What, then, is Wanangwa's cultural locus? Is he African? Is he Western? Is he without a cultural base?

BOX 11.2

sustain even modest levels of consumption, but they will continue to linger on the global fringes, abandoning their traditional ways and seething with dismay at the long, slow, and uncertain path to riches. In other ways as well, African traditions have been obviated: religion, culture, peasantry, governance, and animals have all been displaced, replaced, overwhelmed, destroyed, or transformed beyond recognition—generally without the awareness or assent of those who evolved them and without the introduction of suitable replacements. Popular music has changed from the sounds of indigenous instruments to that of battery-powered radios or tape players. Videos enable ethnologists to depict traditional activities for contemporary students with no need for actual participants. Clothing has become "mod." Reading is the latest pulp fiction. And on and on.

4. Politically, Africa may stabilize at a relatively low level (geographically) of organization. The mischief that accompanied Cold War competition has fortunately passed, and fairly coherent pressures predominate in favor of more conventional Western-style systems. If donor states can bring themselves to reward appropriate behavior, we should see more and more stability and openness in Africa. However, the political configurations that are likely to evolve will not be obvious imitations of parliamentary or presidential systems.[10]

In the thirty years that I have intensively observed Africa, there have been ten pieces of unhappy news to every hopeful one. Drought, famine, revolution, and mayhem make up much more of the diet for Western observers of Africa than does the peaceful transition wrought in South Africa or the orderly elections in Zambia. We can accuse the messenger or we can rue the message. For too long we have abused various messengers without reckoning with profound truths about Africa: Africa is culturally unprepared to become modern in the way that many in the West define "modern," especially given the available models. The process of transition will be expensive for all concerned by every measure. If that is the inevitable route to be taken, the sooner we and they get on with it the better, but we and they must be prepared to pay a price.

NOTES

1. My observations from traveling in Africa over twenty-five years would sustain this. There is infrastructure—highways, vehicles, hospitals, universities. All were state of *some* art at one time, but in no more than a very small fraction of cases have these facilities been maintained by the polity which owns them.

2. At the African university where I taught in 1997, one percent of the student body had died the preceding year, presumably from AIDS.

3. I recently purchased a sport coat made in South Africa—a consequence of the lifting of apartheid-era economic sanctions.

4. Repeatedly, visitors report losing their cameras en route to Africa. The logical question they are asked is: "Did you fly through Nairobi?"

5. Unfortunately, the "parking boys," homeless street urchins who in earlier days "located" parking spaces for drivers in the expectation of a few coins, have been replaced by gun-wielding car-jackers who have murdered drivers in broad daylight and stolen their cars as they stop at traffic lights or are immobilized in Nairobi's frequent traffic jams.

6. Other terms that appear are: "decentralization," "consensus," "demand-driven," and "institutional development." For a brief discussion of such issues see *Findings* 15. April 1994, published by Africa Technical Department, World Bank. See also *African Voices*, USAID Bureau for Africa, passim.

7. Teaching a public administration class in an African University, I posited this problem: "Your agency has just received $1 million for an education project. What questions would you ask as you go about determing how to spend the money?" While there were several logical and predictable responses, the one that shocked me into seeing this argument in clear relief was this one: "I don't need to think about it; *they* will tell us what to do."

8. As this is written, antidemocratic behaviors are reported in Zambia in the wake of an attempted coup. Similarly, the first Kabila government which replaced the autocratic Mobutu in Zaire ("Democratic" Republic of the Congo) was far from the obvious improvement Western policymakers must have hoped for.

9. Nothing is simple. I have an African friend, a professor in an American university whose physician husband practices his skills at home, existing on her salary because he cannot charge patients enough to generate a living wage. His dissolute government will not hire his services. The proper course of action for

this dedicated couple is not easily discerned. A Nigerian professor in the United States has termed her situation a "brain gain" for the United States.

10. An interesting legal situation unfolded in Malawi as I was completing this manuscript. A deputy minister was dismissed by the President. In retaliation, he undertook negotiations with the major opposition party. At this point the ruling party sought to have his seat declared vacant on the grounds that he had been elected as a member of the ruling party. However, the judge's ruling—that it is unconstitutional for an individual to hold positions as both parliamentarian and cabinet member—was unexpected. The last has certainly not been heard on this matter, but it illustrates the kinds of issues that arise as a three-year-old system attempts to find a balance between parliamentary and presidential powers, having adopted elements of each without resolving their inherent contradictions.

APPENDIX A

General Data for Selected African States

APPENDIX A
General Data for Selected African States*

State	Life Expectancy	1992 Adult Literacy (women)	1991 GDP p.c. (US$)	Percent Required Calories	Infant Mortality 1960-1992	Development Assistance (Percent GDP)
Angola	45.6	43 (—)	—	80	208>126	$32 (—)
Benin	46.1	25 (18)	1,500	101	185>88	$55 (3.6%)
Botswana	60.3	75 (—)	4,690	100	116>61	$86 (1 8%)
Burkina Faso	47.9	20 (7)	666	95	205>118	$47 (7.1%)
Burundi	48.2	52 (—)	640	85	153>106	$54 (8.4%)
Cameroon	55.3	57 (59)	2,400	93	163>64	$59 (2.5%)
CAR	46.2	40 (18)	641	77	175>105	$56 (8.7%)
Chad	46.9	33 (—)	447	69	195>123	$42 (9.4%)
Congo	51.7	59 (—)	2,800	107	141>83	$48 (1.7%)
Cote d'Ivoire	51.6	56 (—)	1510	122	166>91	$59 (3.9%)
Djibouti	48.3	— (—)	—	—	186>113	$250 (16.6%)
Ethiopia	46.4	— (—)	370	71	175>123	$24 (6.5%)
Gabon	52.9	62 (—)	3,498	107	171>95	$56 (1.6%)
Gambia	44.4	30 (—)	763	103	213>133	$128 (16.8%)
Ghana	55.4	63 (—)	930	91	132>82	$39 (4.2%)
Guinea	43.9	27 (—)	500	100	203>135	$75 (15%)
Kenya	58.6	71 (—)	1,350	86	124>67	$31 (2.3%)
Lesotho	59.8	— (—)	—	93	149>80	$77 (—)
Liberia	54.7	42 (—)	—	97	184>127	$43 (—)
Madagascar	54.9	81 (—)	710	93	220>110	$28 (3.9%)

Malawi	44.6	— (—)	800	87	207>143	$51 (6.4%)
Mali	45.4	36 (14)	480	107	210>160	$45 (9.4)
Mauritania	47.4	35 (—)	962	109	191>118	$98 (10.2%)
Mozambique	46.5	34 (25)	962	77	190>148	$92 (9.6%)
Namibia	58.0	—	2,381	—	146>71	$91 (3.8%)
Niger	45.9	31 (—)	542	98	192>125	$44 (8.1%)
Nigeria	51.9	52	1,360	93	190>97	$3 (2%)
Rwanda	46.5	52	680	80	150>111	$47 (6.9%)
Senegal	48.7	40	1,680	95	172>81	$87 (5.2%)
Sierra Leone	42.4	24	1,020	86	219>144	$31 (3%)
Somalia	46.4	27	7,59	81	175>123	$62 (8.2%)
South Africa	62.2	—	3,885	128	89>53	— (—)
Sudan	51.2	28	1,162	83	170>100	$23 (1.9%)
Swaziland	57.3	—	2506	105	157>74	$62 (2.5%)
Tanzania	51.2	—	570	91	147>103	$48 (8.4%)
Togo	54.4	45	738	99	182>86	$60 (8.1%)
Uganda	42.6	51	1,036	83	133>104	$38 (3.7%)
Zaire	51.6	74	469	97	158>93	$7 (1.5%)
Zambia	45.5	75	1,010	87	135>84	$118 (11.7%)
Zimbabwe	56.1	69	2,160	94	110>59	$69 (3.2%)

Source: ODA 1992, from UNDP.

*Data suggest a circularity to development. There are, of course, many ways to lower infant mortality rates, one of which is by increasing adult literacy rates. As parents are able to read more and to better understand the science of hygiene, etc., they are better able to care for a child. This inevitably lowers the mortality rate and consequently increases the rate of population growth. The search for development strategies must therefore involve discerning which fundamental factors of human behavior will facilitate the desired consequences. Clearly, literacy is one. Contraceptive use is another. Gender equality is another. Identifying these, however, does not assure the ability to implement them in a reasonable time (or ever).

APPENDIX B

Measures of Well-being

APPENDIX B

Measures of Well-being

State	Foreign Investment as Percent of GDP, 1996	Annual Average Private Consumption Growth, Percent	Average Annual GNP Real Growth, 1990–1996	Population Growth Rate, 1990–1996	PPP* 1996 (US$)	Gini Index†
Angola	4.5	-6.7	-5.6	3.1	1,030	—
Benin	0.1	—	1.9	2.9	1,230	—
Botswana	1.5	-5.7	1.3	2.5	7,350	54.6
Burkina Faso	0.0	-0.1	-0.1	2.8	950	—
Burundi	0.1	-5.4	-6.4	2.6	590	—
Cameroon	0.4	-5.6	-3.8	2.9	1,760	—
CAR	0.5	-2.1	-1.7	2.2	880	—
Chad	1.5	-2.3	-1.7	2.5	880	—
Congo	0.3	2.5	-4.3	2.9	1,410	—
Cote d'Ivoire	0.2	-2.6	0.2	3.0	1,580	44.7
Djibouti	1.0	—	—	3.0	—	—
Eritrea	—	—	—	2.7	—	—
Ethiopia	0.1	-2.3	2.0	2.2	500	32.6
Gabon	-1.1	-4.9	-1.2	2.6	6,300	—
Gambia	2.2	3.4	-0.5	3.7	1,280	—
Ghana	1.9	0.7	1.5	2.7	1,790	36.9
Guinea	0.6	1.7	1.9	2.7	1,720	—
Guinea-Bissau	0.4	4.9	0.5	2.1	1,030	56.2
Kenya	0.1	0.4	-0.5	2.6	1,130	54.7
Lesotho	3.2	-5.0	0.9	2.1	2,380	56.2
Liberia	—	—	—	2.4	—	—
Madagascar	0.2	-2.0	-2.0	2.7	900	—

Country					PPP	Gini
Malawi	0.0	−1.0	−0.2	2.7	690	65.0
Mali	0.9	−1.7	−0.2	2.8	710	—
Mauritania	0.5	−1.4	1.7	2.5	1,810	—
Mozambique	1.7	−2.6	2.6	4.0	500	—
Namibia	4.2	1.5	1.6	2.6	5,390	—
Niger	0.0	—	−2.3	3.3	920	44.0
Nigeria	4.3	0.2	1.2	2.9	870	28.9
Rwanda	0.1	−4.6	−8.2	−0.6	630	—
Senegal	0.9	−1.3	−0.6	2.5	1,650	54.1
Sierra Leone	0.5	−1.3	−3.9	2.4	510	—
Somalia	—	—	—	2.1	—	—
South Africa	0.1	−0.1	−0.2	1.7	7,450	—
Sudan	—	—	—	2.1	—	—
Swaziland	1.2	—	−1.2	3.1	3,320	—
Tanzania	2.6	−0.8	−0.2	3.0	—	59.2
Togo	0.0	−1.9	−3.9	3.0	1,650	—
Uganda	2.0	3.6	4.0	3.2	1,030	33.0
Zaire	0.0	−9.9	−10.4	3.2	790	—
Zambia	1.7	−7.1	−4.8	2.8	860	43.5
Zimbabwe	0.8	0.1	−1.1	2.4	2,200	56.9

Sources: *World Bank Atlas, 1998.*

*PPP = purchasing power parity. This is a measure of the amount of goods and services one can obtain by exchanging U.S. dollars for the currency of a given state. Put differently, in Angola $1,030 in local currency would purchase the equivalent of $1,030 spent in the United States.

†Data are for various dates 1985–1992 from World Bank sources. Gini index measures the disparity of wealth within a society; the higher the number, the greater the disparity.

APPENDIX C

African Financial Data

APPENDIX C
African Financial Data

	Consumer Prices (in hundreds of 1990 dollars)	Unemployment Percent	Imports, 1995–1996 (Various Currencies)	Exports	Balance	IMF Quota
Algeria	409	23.8[d]	171[h]	243	+29	409
Benin	176	—	223[g]	90.5	-146	176
Botswana	36.6	—	4993[h]	5940	+15.9	36.6
Burkina Faso	148	27[c]	213[g]	267	+20.2	44.2
Burundi	195	7[c]	51[g]	26	-119	57.2
Cameroon	158	—	56, 3[g]	1,018	+944	135
CAR	140	6[d]	80[g]	85	+5.9	41
Chad	168	—	81[g]	126	+35.7	41
Congo	217	—	272[g]	585	+53.5	57.0
Cote d'Ivoire	162	—	493c,[g]	751[c]	+34.3	238
Djibouti	—	—	38, 9[c, g]	28[(cif)]	-35.7	11.5
Egypt	209	—	35.9[h]	11	-226	678
Eq. Guinea	119	—	22.2[g]	43	+48.4	24
Ethiopia	178	—	4,770[h]	2,062	-131	98
Gabon	144	—	363[g]	1,354	+73.2	110
Gambia	141	—	1,148[h]	155	-640	23
Ghana	495	41	889[h]	547[c]	-62.5	274
Guinea	—	—	—	—	—	79
Guinea-Bissau	1,249	—	1,102[h]	422	-161	10.5
Kenya	333	—	133[h]	97	-37	199

Country					
Lesotho	200	—	3,448[h]	5,811	+40.6	24
Liberia	—	—	—	3,154	—	71
Libya	—	—	1,355[h]	1,554	+57	818
Madagascar	345	—	1,887[g]	2,805	-21.4	90
Malawi	566	—	2,558[h]	91	+88	51
Mali	148	—	133[g]	24	-24	69
Mauritania	142	—	—	—	—	47
Mauritius	154	8	31.6[h]	40.2	-31.7	73
Morocco	138	16[c]	66.3[h]	169	-64.9	428
Mozambique	802	—	700[i]	4,214	-314	84
Namibia	192	—	3,694[h]	63.7	+12.3	100
Niger	138	21[b]	74.5[g]	206*	-18.4	48
Nigeria	957	—	129[h]	14.7	+37.4	1,282
Rwanda	330	—	43.3[g]	129	-194	59
Senegal	146	10[d]	239[g]	18	85.3	119
Sierra Leone	778	—	91[h]	126	-405	77
South Africa	192	—	129[h]	2,894	-2.7	1,365
Swaziland	219	—	3,636[h]	441	-25.6	36
Tanzania	425	—	684[h]	104	-55	147
Togo	101	—	165[g]	446	-58.6	54
Uganda	272	—	923[h]	438	-106.9	134
Zaire	2,254[b]	—	342[i]	129	+21.9	291
Zambia	3,902	—	144[h]	—	-11.6	263
Zimbabwe	430	—	15.9[h]	15.3	-3.9	261

Sources: *International Financial Statistics*, March, 1997. Data are for 1995–1996 unless noted. Many figures are rounded.

*of which 200 is petroleum

a = 1990 data, b = 1991, c = 1992, d = 1993, e = 1994, g = billion francs, h = local currency, j = US$

Selected References

An effort has been made to keep these references to a minimum—listing only those volumes worth consulting in their entirety to enhance your understanding of Africa. Some are among the classics of African "understanding." Other significant sources have been footnoted. In this Internet age, it seems futile to offer a topic-by-topic list of references. Readers are directed to a favorite Internet search site or to a library catalogue to pursue specific interests.

This volume has drawn lightly from a 1980 volume by this author, *Africa Faces the World* (Arlington, VA: Carrollton Press), so references to that work have been omitted.

Abraham, Willie. 1963. *The Mind of Africa*. Chicago: University of Chicago Press. An African philosopher presents ideas about Africa as it faces a world ignorant of its intellectual roots.

Achebe, Chinua. 1958. *Things Fall Apart*. Greenwich, CN: Fawcett. This classic novel addresses the impact of the missionary presence in West Africa.

———. 1987. *Anthills of the Savannah*. Nairobi: Heinemann Kenya, Ltd. The Nigerian novelist indicts the misrule of a fictional state.

Ake, Claude. 1981. *A Political Economy of Africa*. Harlow, Essex, England: Longman Group, Ltd. A Nigerian scholar offers an early look at the political economy of Africa.

Apter, David E., and Carl G. Rosberg, eds. 1994. *Political Devolvement and the New Realism in Sub-Saharan Africa*. Charlottesville: University of Virginia Press. Collected essays offer theoretical perspectives on African development.

Ayittey, George N. 1992. *Africa Betrayed*. New York: St. Martin's Press. An African economist criticizes exploitation by African leaders.

Benson, Mary. 1994. *Nelson Mandela: The Man and the Movement*. New York: W. W. Norton & Co. A white South African delivers a hopeful biography of Africa's preeminent politician.

Berg, Robert J., and Jennifer Seymour Whitaker, eds. 1986. *Strategies for African Development*. Berkeley: University of California Press. Essays respond to the deepening economic and political crises besetting Africa in the 1980s.

Chazan, Naomi, et al. 1999. *Politics and Society in Contemporary Africa*, 3d ed. Boulder, CO: Lynne Reinner Publishers. A theoretical look at contemporary Africa.

Dia, Mamadou. 1960. *The African Nations and World Solidarity.* New York: Frederick A. Praeger, Inc. One of the original statesmen of African independence sets out a political manifesto.

Diamond, Jared. 1997. *Guns, Germs, and Steel: The Fates of Human Societies.* New York: W.W. Morton.

Fatton, Robert, Jr. 1995. "Africa in the Age of Democratization: The Civic Limitations of Civil Society." *African Studies Review* 38: 2.

Fredland, Richard. 1990. *A Guide to African International Organizations.* London: Hans Zell Publishers. This reference book identifies the many regional organizations that have come and gone in Africa.

Fukuyama, Francis. 1992. *The End of History and the Last Man.* New York: Free Press. A prescription for the post-Cold War world.

Gordimer, Nadine. 1979. *Burger's Daughter.* New York: Viking Press. A white South African novelist shows *apartheid* in practice.

Gordon, April A., and Donald L. Gordon. 1992. *Understanding Contemporary Africa.* Boulder, CO: Lynne Rienner Publishers. The authors take a theoretical look at Africa in the world system.

Harbeson, John W., and Donald Rothchild. 1991. *Africa in World Politics.* Boulder, CO: Westview Press. This textbook examines Africa in the larger world.

Hazelwood, Arthur. 1975. *Economic Integration: The East African Experience.* New York: St. Martin's Press. A British economist thoroughly examines the most complete example to date of integration in Africa.

Hochschild, Adam. 1998. *King Leopold's Ghost.* Boston: Houghton Mifflin Co.

Huntington, Samuel P. 1996. *The Clash of Civilizations and the Remaking of World Order.* New York: Simon and Schuster. A description of the post-Cold War world.

Johns, Sheridan, and R. Hunt Davis Jr. 1991. *Mandela, Tambo, and the African National Congress.* New York: Oxford University Press. The authors present a detailed examination of the ANC.

Kaplan, Robert D. 1996. *The Ends of the Earth: A Journey at the Dawn of the 21st Century.* New York: Random House. Kaplan's account of a journey through Africa and Asia offers detailed observations of economic and social conditions.

Kenyatta, Jomo. 1962. *Facing Mount Kenya: The Tribal Life of the Gikuyu.* New York: Random House. Kenyatta wrote this doctoral dissertation for his anthropology degree in London.

Malinowski, Bronislaw. 1961. *The Dynamics of Culture Change: An Inquiry in Race Relations in Africa.* New Haven, CT: Yale University Press. This is one of the first comprehensive anthropological surveys of Africa.

SELECTED REFERENCES

Mandela, Nelson. 1994. *Long Walk to Freedom*. Boston: Little Brown & Co. Mandela's autobiographical and political essay demonstrates the equanimity with which he faced unparalleled difficulties.

Markowitz, Irving Leonard. 1977. *Power and Class in Africa*. Englewood Cliffs, NJ: Prentice-Hall, Inc. Markowitz offers a non-Marxist, socioeconomic analysis of Africa's structures several years into independence.

Martin, Phyllis, and Patrick O'Meara. 1986. *Africa*, 2nd ed. Bloomington: Indiana University Press. The authors take a holistic view of Africa from a cultural perspective.

Mazrui, Ali. 1980. *The African Condition*. London: Cambridge University Press. This eclectic statement of Africa's role in a world of growing interdependence is written by Africa's preeminent academic.

Michener, James. 1987. *The Covenant*. New York: Random House. This novel tells a compelling tale, constructing a multifamily history of South Africa.

Mittelman, James H. 1988. *Out from Underdevelopment*. New York: St. Martin's Press. The author considers developing areas and the issues affecting them from the perspective of improving, not just describing, their situations.

Naipaul, V. S. 1979. *A Bend in the River*. New York: Random House. A Caribbean novelist looks at the life of expatriate traders in Zaire.

Ngugi wa Thiongo. 1977. *Petals of Blood*. New York: E. P. Dutton. A Kenyan novelist reveals his country's dysfunctional system.

Nyerere, Julius. 1968. *Ujamaa: Essays on Socialism*. Dar Es Salaam: Oxford University Press. The conceptual founder of African socialism offers this classical statement of his political philosophy.

Palmer, Monte. 1989. *Dilemmas of Political Development*. Itasca, IL: F.E. Peacock.

Said, Abdul Aziz. 1966. *The African Phenomenon*. Boston: Allyn and Bacon Inc. Said presents an early international political view of the continent.

Steele, Ronald. 1995. *Temptations of a Superpower*. Cambridge: Harvard University Press.

Soyinka, Wole. 1996. *The Open Sore of a Continent*. New York: Oxford University Press. Soyinka, who was executed in 1995, relates the decline of Nigeria in personal terms.

Tordoff, William. 1993. *Government and Politics in Africa*. Bloomington: Indiana University Press. This basic textbook takes a political perspective.

Ungar, Sanford J. 1989. *Africa: The People and Politics of an Emerging Continent*, 3d ed. New York: Simon & Schuster. The political travelogue crosses Africa, country by country.

Wallerstein, Immanuel. 1991. *Geopolitics and Geoculture: Essays on the Changing World System*. Cambridge, England: Cambridge University Press. The author examines the place of Africa in the world.

Wiseman, Jon A. 1990. *Democracy in Black Africa*. New York: Paragon House Publishers. A British scholar presents a theoretical and practical examination of democracy in Africa.

Young, Crawford. 1982. *Ideology and Development in Africa*. New Haven: Yale University Press. A renowned U.S. scholar looks at the role of ideology in African politics.

GENERAL SOURCES

Journals, Magazines, and Periodicals

African Affairs
African Studies Review (journal of the African Studies Association)
Africa Report
Africa Today
Journal of African History
Journal of Modern African Studies

Reference Books

Africa South of the Sahara, Europa Yearbooks
Human Development Report (annual), United Nations Development Report
World Development Report (annual), The World Bank

INTERNET SITES

<africanews.org> for information from the African News Service
<allAfrica.com>
<caster.ssw.upenn.edu> for information about social and economic development issues
<igc.org/igc/index.html> for information from the Institute for Global Communications (human rights)
<mailbase.ac.uk> for information about forced migration
<nyt.com>
<oneworld.org/iai/info.htm>
<overt.org> for information about AIDS
<washingtonpost.com/>

Index

Page numbers in boldface indicate references in tables or figures.

INDEX

INDEX

Photo Credits